The History of OCR
Optical Character Recognition

Herbert F. Schantz

Published by the Recognition Technologies Users Association

Library of Congress Catalogue Card Number: 82-60600

ISBN Number: 0-943072-01-8

Acknowledgements

The author would like to thank the members and directors of the Recognition Technology Users Association whose support and guidance made this book possible. He would like to offer special thanks to Richard "Buck" Burns whose encouragement and management skills kept this project on schedule. Special thanks are also offered to Franklin Cooper and Dean Huffman who initiated this project many years ago. The author is indebted to Elliott Kagen who helped with the initial draft. However, it was the OCR pioneers whose accomplishments are chronicled in this text who were the real inspiration of this research. And last but not least, the long nights and weekends by Dr. L. M. Schantz in editing, rewriting, and typing this manuscript are greatly appreciated.

This book is the combined effort of many people who I have been fortunate enough to know and work with over a long period of time. A group who have by their foresight and leadership made this work possible . . . The OCR Users.

HERBERT F. SCHANTZ

Dedication

This book is dedicated to my wife Letty Lou whose support, intellect, and dedication made this book possible.

HFS

Contents

Chapter 1   Men of Vision   1

Chapter 2   OCR's ''Fabulous Fifties''   7

Chapter 3   Years of Expansion   15

Chapter 4   The ''Eyes'' of Texas 1961–69   23

Chapter 5   Sales, Service and Standardization   31

Chapter 6   ''Why Should I Use OCR?''   41

Chapter 7   A Mature Technology 1970–80   53

Chapter 8   OCR In the Age of Instant Response   61

Photographs

Appendix A   OCR List of Terms   67

Appendix B   An OCR Chronology   93

Appendix C   References   101

Guide to Footnotes   105

Index   107

Chapter One

Men of Vision

Optical Character Recognition: Where did it Really Begin?

To answer the question where optical character recognition really began tempts one to be overzealous and to look for OCR's early roots in the well-researched history of mankind's first use of symbols for representing concepts and, later, language. An equal temptation is to probe the dusty archives containing records of the earliest gropings of those scientists and pseudo scientists who long ago sought to define the nature and properties of light. However, comparatively disappointing as it may seem, the first truly discernable steps towards the eventual devlopment of optical character recognition go back less than 200 years, to the first decade of the 19th century and to the efforts of men searching to enhance communication.

In 1809, at a time when the grand armies of Napoleon were conquering much of Europe and Thomas Jefferson was President of the infant United States of America, the first patents for reading devices to aid the blind were awarded. These almost forgotten inventions to help expand the horizons of persons without sight were the first real "seeds" of OCR's development.

After the passage of approximately 60 years, a significant stride in true optical character recognition was reportedly made by C. R. Carey of Boston Massachusetts. He used a mosaic of photocells in an image transmission system. As a result, Carey is credited with the first documented example of what is now known as the "retina scanner."[1]

Two decades later, P. Nipkow of Poland originated the concept of sequential scanning. His ingenious technological development, the "Nipkow Disk," represented a major step in OCR's evolutionary progress. With Nipkow's sequential scanning disk, analyzing images line-by-line was made possible as well as some future innovations. Subsequently, Nipkow's sequential scanning process was used as a principle for the operation of modern television cameras and as a method applied by many contemporary OCR system scanners.[2]

Between the years of 1912 and 1914, when Western Civilization was hurtling towards the cataclysm of the First World War, two of the early OCR pioneers, Emmanuel Goldberg and Edmund Fournier D'Albe, appeared. Though these two men worked independently, Goldberg and Fournier D'Albe may be justifiably credited with the coincidental and almost simultaneous development of devices which, in retrospect, were the first true "readers" or machines that were able to convert printed characters into another format. The print-conversion principles employed by Goldberg and Fournier D'Albe, rather than the purpose of their inventions, were truly significant foundations for the early development of OCR.

Goldberg's work was done in Chicago. In the year of 1912, he patented a machine that directly read characters and converted those symbols into standard telegraph code. His machine read typed messages, converted them to paper tape, and then used the tape to transmit telegraphic messages over wires without human intervention. Thus, Goldberg's major contribution was to telegraphic communication in that translatable "Morse Code" was generated for message transmission to the appropriate points of reception.[3] For early OCR technology, Goldberg's contribution was that of demonstrating a practical application for the conversion of print to a coded format for subsequent translation.

Fournier D'Albe, on the other hand, was primarily concerned with instruments to aid the blind. In 1914, he invented the OCR device called the "Optophone." The Optophone was a handheld scanner which emitted a "meaningful audio output" when moved across a printed page. First demonstrated as early as 1912, the Optophone optically scanned printed material and produced a series of audible tones while being moved along a page. Each produced tone corresponded to a specific letter or character. After learning the character equivalent for the various tones, visually impaired persons were able to "read" and interpret the printed material. As might be imagined, accurate interpretation of tones demanded a great deal of concentration and skill on the part of users. For this reason, the Optophone never experienced widespread use. However, the device was a practical, working application of early OCR scanning technology.

In the late 1920's, two engineers working for the American Telephone and Telegraph Company (AT&T) patented systems which scanned messages and encoded them into "Morse Code" for telegraphic transmission. Like the Optophone, these telegraphic OCR systems never experienced widespread use. However, the AT&T telegraphic transmission system represented an intermediate step in the eventual development of true, OCR technology.

In brief, by the end of the second decade of the 19th century, early attempts to expand the field of telegraphy and to develop devices to aid the blind through precocious experimentation with OCR had convincingly demonstrated the feasibility of optically scanning printed materials, converting that material into electronic code signals, and subsequently uncoding the electronic signals. More importantly, these early inventions and processes furnished a model for later computer-based OCR systems in which data would be encoded into acceptable "computer formats" via optical scanning technique. Reaching that primary objective, data would be stored, recalled for use when needed, and ultimately decoded into another printed format. As a result, the 1930's would predictably be another "bright" era in the search to develop practical, reliable optical character recognition devices despite the darkness created by the Great Depression.

The decade of the thirties began with a continued interest in telegraphic communication and was marked by several notable OCR and related technological accomplishments, especially those applied to statistical processes. In 1931, patents were issued to R. D. Parker and A. Weaver for telegraph reading machines. That same year and in 1932, "statistical machines" which utilized optical scanning technology were patented by two independent inventors, Emmanuel Goldberg and Paul H. Handel. Both men registered devices for counting and identifying statistical records through optical pattern matching.

Many current sophisticated OCR systems trace their lineage directly from these early inventions.

Goldberg, already known for the invention of OCR-type telegraphic devices, suggested in the late-1920's that statistical equipment could productively apply optical scanning technology for a form of "data entry." He proposed photographing data records for reading and that the resultant photographic-record transparencies could then be matched against a negative "template" or "search plate" containing the desired identification pattern. He further hypothesized that once a match was located, the coincidence of pattern would cause a light source to be completely blocked from a detection device, more specifically, a photographic cell. Goldberg's 1931 patent was for such a device.

In 1932, a patent was issued to P. W. Handel for a statistical device which, like Goldberg's, interpreted data by means of photoelectric detection of light blockage. Handel's patented invention compared a source pattern with a series of stencil patterns maintained on a rotating disk. Because of the methodologies employed by Handel and Goldberg, the critical technique of "template-matching" was born. Ultimately, this principle proved to be the basic technique applied in the first, actual-working character readers which were to appear in the early 1950's.

A critical drawback for the early template-matching devices

was their limited degree of accuracy. Difficulties in precisely aligning source patterns with template patterns or improper alignment inevitably resulted in extraneous light passing through the template, even when a character match occurred. During the next twenty years, a number of attempts were made to resolve problems with optical template-matching devices. Many variations of the original concept were conceived and tried. And, records indicate that, during this period, a large number of patents were issued to European inventors for template-matching inventions.

The year 1938 was a significant one in the early annals of OCR history for two reasons. First, International Business Machines Corporation (IBM) entered the optical scanning field. Second, young Jacob Rabinow was introduced.

Waldemar Ayres, assignor to IBM, was awarded the patent for a "Light Sensitive Device" in 1938. After this initial patent entry, IBM's engineering staff continued their OCR and related research efforts throughout the 1940's and 1950's. Periodically, during those years, patents were earned for various OCR-type achievements. However, IBM made no attempt to market commercial optical character recognition devices until after 1960.

That same year, 1938, Jacob C. Rabinow, who was later to play an integral role in the development of OCR technology, entered the challenging field of OCR research which was already exhibiting some of its vast potential for future applications. Rabinow aptly described the experimental conditions at that time of his introduction to OCR stating, "There was a flurry of work in the 1930's on the conversion of visual images (particularly characters) into tactile or sound outputs as aids to the blind. This is how I became involved in 1938. Louis Braille, in his original work, experimented with characters embossed on paper. He soon abandoned this for the six-bit binary code almost universally used today."[4]

The development and refining of optical character reading techniques continued to move ahead throughout the 1940's. Perhaps most notable during this decade was Radio Corporation of

America's (RCA) effort to develop reading devices to aid the blind. By 1946, RCA developed an "electric pencil" which performed or improved upon many functions of the Optophone produced thirty-two years earlier by D'Albe. The RCA development was also more compact than its 1914 predecessor. Despite such improvements, devices such as the electric pencil never experienced widespread use by the handicapped population.

These progressive, well-intentioned innovations did, however, add significantly to the expanding body of knowledge which formed the nucleus for subsequent development of practical OCR technology. For example, as early as 1948, the noted expert, Mortimer Taube, suggested that signals produced from electric pencils could be coupled with facsimile devices for transmitting the content of printed pages to remote terminals.

In conclusion, during this 130 year evolution of early, exploratory experimentation with various OCR techniques, OCR's application as a viable means for data entry did not become a reality.

However, with the birth of the electronic data processing industry in the mid-1940's the need for a data entry methodology became significant, particularly throughout the business world.[5] The foundations for that data entry methodology were laid by these men of vision and their inventions. Subsequent pioneers attempted to address the business world's need in OCR's decade of the fabulous fifties.

Chapter Two

OCR's
"Fabulous Fifties"

By the year 1950, the 20th century's "Technological Revolution" had begun to move forward at an overwhelming speed, with a seemingly limitless range of new and better developments occurring almost before their antecedents could be marketed and used widely. The fledgling computer industry had already established a firm toehold throughout the American business community. Moreover, the future predominence of computers was clearly apparent to those scientists, technologists and businesspeople who had a clear perspective of the experimental work which had been done and which was continuing in the field of electronic data processing.

Unit record equipment to process information coded on punched cards was, by the mid-century, gaining wide acceptance and use. However, a need existed for a cost-effective way to handle the constantly expanding volume of "data" used in the commercial and scientific communities. In many of these areas of endeavor, Perceptive individuals foresaw a continuing and astonishing growth rate for data volume.

At the same time, the technology to create an electronic machine capable of "seeing" and "recognizing" written or printed patterns had evolved to the point where its application to the data processing field was possible. Recognition and discrimination techniques had been identified for optically scanning and reading print primarily through the use of hardware circuitry. The concept of applying optical character recognition to business-oriented tasks such as statistical accounting had also been hypothesized and, in some situations, prototype systems had been built. In addition, workable output modes such as audible tone creation, punched card formats and direct print output to typewriter-like devices had been constructed and demonstrated. The time for the productive, practical development, and use of some true optical character recognition systems was now at hand.

On Friday, April 27, 1951, the Washington Daily News printed a short feature under the headline, "Electric Brain in the Attic: Falls Church Man's 'GISMO' Is A Robot Reader-Writer". This provocative but non-scientific article heralded the public introduction of David Shepard's "home-made" scanning device— a device which he nicknamed "Gismo".

Shepard, who was a 27-year-old research scientist working for the Department of Defense when "Gismo" made its debut, had created an invention capable of reading 23 letters of the alphabet, which had been produced by a standard typewriter. While "Gismo" was by no means the first working optical scanner and even though the device did not in any way represent the creation of a truly "practical" or "intelligent" scanner, Shepard's invention clearly captured press attention and brought OCR's prospects and possibilities some well-deserved public recognition.

Shepard, aided by his friend Harvey Cook, had indeed created an interesting machine in the attic of his Virginia home. "Gismo" performed a variety of functions: It could comprehend Morse Code, read musical notations and even read aloud from printed pages. As reported at the time, if a blind person inserted a page of printed material into the machine, "Gismo" was able to read the content back to him letter by letter. Shepard's machine also duplicated typewritten pages. NEA Special Correspondent Jack Olsen quoted Shepard as saying that once "Gismo" got into production, the machine would have about 99.9 percent reading accuray and would sell for approximately $1000.00.

While the capabilities and costs of optical character recognition systems have come a long way since the introduction of "Gismo," David Shepard's invention may in many ways be credited with igniting the "spark" that generated the first widespread awareness that the Computer Age required and demanded OCR as one practical method of data entry. In retrospect, clearly the development of "Gismo" represented the culmination of only one of many experimental efforts relating to optical recognition that were underway in the late 1940's and early 1950's. However, the significance of Shepard's invention was not kept secret in an access-restricted corporate laboratory or a government research facility. Thus the appearance of "Gismo" and the resulting publicity made a major impact on the OCR-related development industry.

"Gismo" demonstrated that developing a relatively inexpensive, operating reader was possible and attracted many interested, potential users from various areas of government and business. In effect, this machine established the first potential commercial marketplace for OCR technology and equipment. The combination of these factors and the increasing interest in OCR shown by potential systems manufacturers helped to accelerate those efforts already in progress, and to stimulate new developmental efforts.

Shortly after "Gismo" grabbed the public's attention, Shepard founded Intelligent Machines Research Corporation (IMR). This innovative technologist was now personally proceeding in earnest to develop and apply OCR technology to commercial data processing's problems and needs. Subsequently, in 1953, a patent was issued to David Shepard for his "Apparatus for Reading."

Jacob Rabinow built his initial reading machine at about this same time that Shepard and IMR were making their first entries into the commercial OCR industry. Rabinow succinctly described his efforts during this period in his indispensable OCR historical/technological volume, which is wryly titled *Sense and Nonsense*:

". . . I started serious work on OCR in about 1949 because of some work on Dr. Vannevar Bush's 'Rapid Selector.' This was a 35 millimeter film processor where data, recorded on film, had to be identified by a dot code accompanying each record. The dot code had to be recognized 'on-the-fly' at about 300 frames per second and the original design of the Rapid Selector, understandably, had some difficulties. . . . In working on the recognition of the dot pattern, it occurred to me that recognizing a pattern of dots is basically no different from recognizing a character and that, in order to take care of misregistrations, noise, and other imperfections, some sophistication in the pattern matching device was necessary. Thus, the best match technique was born. . . ."[6]

"Jack" Rabinow continued his diligent research and efforts, moving on past the capabilities of the "Rapid Selector" and building a prototype optical reader in 1952 at the Diamond Ordnance Fuze Laboratories (DOFL) in collaboration with the National Bureau of Standards. This prototype reader read upper case alphanumeric characters generated by a portable typewriter at the "fantastic" speed of one character per minute! The machine has since been exhibited at the Smithsonian Institute in Washington, D.C.[7]

By 1954, Rabinow had gained confidence in both the potential of OCR and his own knowledge of optical recognition techniques. He left the National Bureau of Standards to establish Rabinow Engineering, a company devoted to building OCR machines. He described this endeavor as follows: "Here, we designed and built a wide variety of equipment for reading both conventional and unconventional characters, characters in upper and lower case, and machines to read handprinted characters. We designed many special machine-readable characters . . ."

He continued, "I believe we have also used all of the known methods of scanning: discs, retinas, columns and rows of photocells, cathode rays and lasers. We have moved photocells, mirrors, lenses and, of course, paper. We have used total area correlation, feature analysis, curve tracing and many other techniques. We have used noise filtering, image pre-processing and other such aids."[8]

Ultimately, Rabinow sold his company and patent rights to Control Data Corporation. Control Data then used the achievements of Rabinow and his colleagues to form the basis for eventually developing a line of optical recognition devices. Subsequently, Jack Rabinow became a Control Data vice president, responsible for operations at the Rabinow Laboratory Division of that company. Recognized widely over the ensuing years for his pioneering achievements in OCR technology, more recently Rabinow has also advised the United States Postal Service on the design and installation of mail scanning and sorting systems.[9]

A major plateau in OCR's progress was reached with the milestone Reader's Digest installation in Pleasantville, New York in the year 1954. The Reader's Digest machine was the first actual installation of a commercial OCR reader in a business environment. This initial IMR equipment at Reader's Digest was used to convert typewritten documents (sales reports) into punched cards for input into the computer in the magazine's subscription department.[10]

Reader's Digest is now justifiably acknowledged as the "Pioneer User" of optical scanning equipment, having employed a character reader since September, 1955 to process shipments of from 15 to 20 million books each year. The equipment has enabled Reader's Digest to reduce order processing time from the former rate of one month to a little more than a day. The Reader's Digest scanner is often cited as "paying for itself" twice each year and by September of 1959, had already read its billionth character.

IMR's progress and technological achievements in the burgeoning OCR field continued throughout the fifties. In 1956, IMR equipment for scanning petroleum charge cards was sold by Farrington Manufacturing to Standard Oil of California. Subsequently, this equipment was put into operation at Standard Oil's facilities in Salt Lake City, Utah. During that same year, IMR licensed Shepherd's inventions to IBM, whose interest in OCR had been continuing since the late 1930's. In 1959, IMR built an "analyzing" reader for the United States Post Office and also installed the first prototype OCR page reader in Rome, New York for the use of the United States Air Force. The later machine, the analyzing reader, had the capability of reading a full upper and lower case alpha-numeric font.[11]

The culmination of IMR's contributions to the OCR industry occurred in March of 1959, when IMR merged its manufacturing operations with those of Farrington Manufacturing. Dealings between these companies began in 1954 when Farrington bought the first "Scandex" Equipment (trade name for its OCR reader) from IMR. In this merger, David Shepherd became vice president of research and development with Farrington, and later served as a consultant to IBM during that company's early experimentation with magnetic ink character recognition (MICR) technology. Eventually, Dr. Shepherd became the president of Cognitronics, Incorporated.

OCR's "Fabulous Fifties" were by no means confined to the noteworthy achievements of Shepherd and Rabinow. Mail-sorting held a great deal of potential and challenge for successful OCR applications. In 1953, Maurice M. Levy cooperated with the Post Office of Canada in using various types of reading machines in that nation's mail-sorting operations.

The decade was also marked by many other notable accomplishments and, perhaps even more important, the widespread realization of the need for various OCR-related standardizations. In 1954, M. L. Greenough and C. C. Gordon built the demonstration model of a reader for typewritten characters in the electronic instrumentation section of the National Bureau of Standards. In 1957, Bell Laboratories demonstrated its "STYLATOR"—a stylus recording device for reading numerical hand-printed characters drawn by the company's toll call operators. And, in 1959, Control Instruments Company, a subsidiary of Burroughs, developed the typed page reader (AN/FST6) for the United States Army Signal Corps.

Clearly, optical recognition devices influenced an impressive, wide range of commercial and government markets, during this period, and made significant strides in the essential corollary area of standardization. According to Rabinow, "It became very apparent, early in 1950, that when reading machines became numerous, they would have to read documents generated not only by their owners, but paper generated by others as well . . . I am talking here not only of the OCR machines but of the printers, paper, ink and everything else involved."[12] In 1954, Rabinow's group issued a "Report on Standardization of the 5 × 7 Font," a report proposing that standard characters be designed for OCR machine use. (Note: The characters referred to were based on the 5 × 7 grid used by many companies at that time.)[13]

Rabinow was not alone in his perceptive realization that if optical scanning was to proliferate and reach its productive potential a pressing need existed for various standardizations. In 1956, the American Bankers Association recommended the standard adoption of magnetic ink for high-speed machine automatic character recognition. Shortly thereafter, the Research Institute of the National Retail Merchants Association formed an optical scanning standards committee. In turn, this committee subsequently recommended the adoption of optical recognition systems, rather than magnetic character systems, for standard application throughout the American retail merchandising industry.

As the 1950's drew to a close, OCR had definitely asserted itself as a viable means for meeting many data entry needs in numerous areas of the growing data processing environment. The apparent and limitless prospects for OCR applications as well as the requirement for OCR standardization were very evident. Optical scanning had a firmly established place in the minds of many scientists, technologists and potential users. Moreover, farsighted businessmen quickly perceived the vast prospects for the industry's growth and the profitable marketing of reliable optical scanning systems.

In sum, OCR's infancy and childhood were over. A dynamic era of growth was about to begin.

Chapter Three

Years of Expansion

Optical scanning's promise and potential became apparent by the year 1960. Insight into the direction of OCR technology and applications appeared in "Management and Business Automation" in September of that year in an article prophetically entitled "Optical Scanning—An Unlimited Horizon":

"Commercial optical scanning is the 'real world' of but one manufacturer—Farrington Electronics—which acquired the 'EYE' reading machines through a merger with Intelligent Machines Research Corporation in March of 1959." "IBM, General Electric (GE), RCA and National Cash Register (NCR) are among those expected to announce their entry into the optical scanning field at any moment. The National Data Processing Company of Dallas, Texas, has announced plans to install the first optical scanning system to handle retail accounts receivable. Called the NDP 'Readatron', the system is expected to be installed in a large Southern department store later this year."

"Addressograph-Multigraph has perfected its optical code scanner which operates on a 'bar code' principle: the scanner reads the codes which are printed above the characters rather than reading the actual character. The company has introduced the system in the oil industry, and is planning a concentrated attack on department store accounting functions where the Addressograph plastic credit card would be the key to the system input . . .''

"But while others are developing or announcing, Farrington (i.e. through its merger with IMR) has a long list of successful and satisfied customers with some 29 scanners in operation with 15 firms. Included on the list are: First National City Bank, New York (processing travellers' checks); National Biscuit Company, New York (converting sales records to cards); Reader's Digest, Pleasantville, New York (book club record processing); American Telephone and Telegraph Compay (dividend checks and stockholder records); Ohio Bell Telephone, Cleveland, Ohio; Arizona Public Service Company, Phoenix, Arizona; and Atlantic City Electric Company, Atlantic City, New Jersey (cash accounting)."

Additional insight into OCR's progress and prospects for the sixties was offered by Arnold Keller, the highly respected editor of "Infosystems". In 1960 he wrote, "The only apparent limitation factor to the widespread use of optical scanning in the business world . . . is the necessity, at present, to custom-build equipment for specific applications. This necessarily keeps the production costs per machine at a high figure."

Keller, a perceptive writer and data processing industry spokesman, was correct. During the 1960's, the use of optical scanning systems expanded greatly throughout the business world. Moreover, most of the equipment used was comparatively expensive and systems were custom-built. (Note: Twenty years after Keller's statements, the challenge to build more versatile, less-expensive, standardized OCR systems persisted. Some manufacturers made significant strides in relegating optical scanning's traditionally customized, costly "dinosaurs" to an "extinct" status.)

The early trend to build custom OCR machines was the result of commercial activity in two major areas. First, large corporations with financial resources available for investment in expensive capital equipment subsidized the design and manufacture of custom machines for specific internal applications. Second, government agencies, using available budgets, actively pursued the application of optical scanning for their agencies' specific purposes. Those government agencies and entities supporting OCR developmental efforts during this period included the National Bureau of Standards, the U.S. Post Office Department, the Civil Service Commission, the U.S. Air Force and, to varying degrees, the other branches of the Armed Forces.

Especially noteworthy was the involvement of the U.S. Post Office with OCR. Postal officials at many levels perceived OCR technology as a productive solution to at least one persistent problem: mail routing, the sorting of incoming mail into batches by geographical region.

OCR's answer to the postal problem encompassed searching envelopes for the mailing address. When found, an address was optically recognized and then sorted into common destination batches. Previously, the painstaking sorting process used by the Post Office demanded a rigorous training program for the postal clerks, who had to memorize destination codes and manually key these codes for each individual piece of mail. Postal officials estimated that enormous savings could be realized in both time and labor if only half of the incoming mail was accurately sorted through automation employing optical character recognition.

The Post Office, therefore, employed not only government staff engineers but also many private corporations to develop a viable solution to this situation. Farrington, Philco-Ford, Burroughs and the Rabinow Engineering Division of Control Data Corporation were among the companies actively involved in this quest to solve postal problems using OCR.

Optical character recognition also made a widespread, tangible impact on the commercial world of electronic data processing during the 1960-70 decade. So rapid was the growth of OCR during this ten-year span that, by 1970, there were approximately 50 different manufacturers offering more than 100 different models of commercial OCR machines and systems. A review of the technological advances in optical scanning's maturation process that took place during the 1960's and which were to have a far-reaching impact on the subsequent development and applications of OCR follows.

Throughout the decade, a variety of different detection systems were developed which significantly improved the accuracy of pattern detection. These developments had two major effects upon the OCR industry: first, very reliable readers were manufactured and offered commercially; and, second, readers were built to detect almost any consistently formed character patterns.

Electronic innovations such as the development of transistors allowed less expensive readers to be built. Transistorized readers were more compact and more efficient than their earlier predecessors. Software and hardware refinements were progressively made in the recognition process. The key effect of these refinements was the potential to construct multifont optical readers with the capability of recognizing any of a number of font styles that might appear on documents.

Major improvements and new developments were also made in the essential corollary technology of "transport" design. Readers designed with these new transport features handled pages as large as nine inches by fourteen inches, or documents (i.e. miscellaneous pieces of paper) as small as two inches by three inches. Greater transport capabilities for document-handling attracted many new users with various and different application challenges for OCR systems.

Finally, as expanding markets became apparent to OCR equipment manufacturers, during this decade, a technological "competitiveness" which produced numerous other OCR innovations resulted. Companies with new entries in the optical scanning equipment spectrum inevitably attempted to outshine their forerunners in terms of technical characteristics such as font capability, transport capability, speed, accuracy, multimedia accessories, editing capabilities and computer system interface versatility.

In brief, the leading edges of commercial OCR technology were continually pushed ahead throughout the 1960's. As a result, equipment manufacturers had to be highly competitive and innovative to stay in the systems marketing contest.

It is also relevant to note here that in March of 1960, a great step forward was taken in the area of font standardization with the establishment of the American Standards Institute (ANSI) X3A1 Committee on automatic data processing. The X3A1 Committee was specifically concerned with the adoption of a standard, stylized font for use with optical character recognition systems. This committee's formation and goals were in themselves a tribute to the fact that OCR had indeed "come of age."

The year 1960 was also marked by noteworthy achievements by four OCR equipment manufacturers. They were Farrington, Philco-Ford, IBM and the National Data Processing Company.

Early in that year, Farrington delivered the first document carrier to the Arizona Public Service Company in Phoenix. This machine incorporated the effective use of vacuum tubes, and represented the forerunner of our contemporary solid state electronics products.[14]

Philco Corporation's research division developed an all-electronic, alpha-numeric, recognition device in 1960. This machine identified typed or printed envelope addresses and was developed specifically for use by the U.S. Post Office. This innovation resulted in the awarding of a contract to Philco for a reader that recognized 75 addresses at the anticipated rate of 1500 characters per second.

IBM, which had been active in OCR technological research and development since the mid-1940's, introduced its "1418" document reader in 1960, a memorable year for optical scanning devices. The "1418" was designed as an input reader used on-line to IBM's 1401 computer.

And, in 1960, Dallas' National Data Processing Company installed the first optical scanning system to be used for the handling of retail accounts receivable. The role of the National Data Processing Company (NDP) was especially important to the history of OCR not only because of contributions to the field, but also because that company introduced another farsighted individual who subsequently asserted his place among the "giants" of optical character recognition, Herman L. Philipson, Jr. Additionally, NDP served as the foundation for the world's most dynamic company in the manufacture, marketing and service of OCR systems, specifically, Recognition Equipment Incorporated.

Philipson, a Dallas native, established National Data Processing in 1957 as a high technology company primarily concerned with the development of data processing equipment. Previously, Philipson studied engineering at Texas A&M University in College Station and after service as an infantry officer in the U.S. Army, returned to Dallas to manage a family-owned specialty store.

In addition to other endeavors, NDP's comparatively small staff became heavily involved with developing and perfecting a system to create an imprinted bar code on credit card receipts. This bar code, in turn, was to be read optically to determine basic information from transaction receipts. Using the resultant technological developments as a basis, NDP's staff proceeded to build prototype optical scanning readers capable of recognizing characters.

In 1961, National Data Processing was sold to Sperry Rand Division of Univac, which acquired the rights to equipment developed by NDP. However, Philipson, who was NDP's president, did not return to the family business. That same year, he founded Recognition Equipment Incorporated (REI), bringing to that company many of the technologically innovative personnel who had been part of the NDP team.

Efforts of REI were immediately directed towards the progress and prospects of OCR. Throughout the decade, REI logged many technological achievements and marketing successes which set a fast pace in the industry. Before detailing the evolution of this

OCR company, noteworthy accomplishments of a few other out-standing OCR-oriented companies in the early 1960's are described.

In 1961, National Cash Register installed the first production model of a journal tape reader. This important innovation became a model for OCR applications involving journal tapes produced by adding machines, cash registers, and other devices that produced printed numerical records on roll paper. The net effect was a "captive" market, using OCR, since accounting systems were manufactured which allowed automatic, optical reading of the printed data on these tape rolls. These journal tape readers may be considered the ancestors of point-of-sale OCR systems that were so very popular in the retail environment during the late 1970's.

During the period of 1961-62, IBM displayed an experimental, constrained handwritten character recognition device at the Western Joint Computer Conference; and, RCA demonstrated an OCR machine using optical correlation and matching for reading Cluneve type at its Princeton, New Jersey laboratories. Furthermore, OCR research in the early 1960's was not restricted to those companies either primarily or peripherally concerned with optical scanning equipment. For instance, in 1961, General Motors initiated a long-range program in OCR pattern and character recognition at the Technical Center's research laboratories in Warren, Michigan.

In 1962, the Rabinow Engineering Company demonstrated a machine which possessed the capability of recognizing handprinted characters optically. That same year, this company installed its first commercial OCR data entry system at the Ryder Trucking Company in Florida. The device's applications involved reading typed waybills, those documents prepared by Ryder listing the details of shipments, routes and charges. This particular machine read two lines of numerical data simultaneously.[15] As mentioned earlier, Control Data Corporation was soon to acquire Rabinow Engineering Company and the rights to its OCR developments.

From 1962 through 1965, the annals of OCR's history are dominated by the wide scope of achievements attained by Herman Philipson and his colleagues at Recognition Equipment. Although many other high technology companies continued to develop and market their own OCR-based systems with varying degrees of success throughout the remainder of the 1960's and 1970's, REI's predominance in the optical character recognition field was to continue unabated, at least until 1980, when the company revised and expanded its charter to encompass other state-of-the-art technologies along with OCR.

Chapter Four

The "Eyes" of Texas 1961-69

November 2, 1961 five people gathered together in a building, located near downtown Dallas, that had previously been used as a funeral home. Sitting on the floor around a card table, the only "furniture" in the new company's headquarters, they talked and worked keeping on their coats, since there was no heat in the building, and ending their first workday at dusk, since there were no lights. However, the spirits and enthusiasm of these five intrepid individuals—Herman Philipson, Gordon Perry, Fred Davies, Jessica Eads and Barbara Smith—were not dampened by their stark surroundings. They were buoyant with energy and bubbling over with ideas because their tiny new company, Recognition Equipment, had become a reality, and the time was at hand to start putting their ideas into action.

The primary goal of Philipson and his closely knit group of former National Data Processing Company employees was to develop new, more efficient ways to enter data into computers. Conventional methods such as keypunching were costly, time-consuming and far too often subject to error. The Recognition staff's idea was to design, manufacture and market the most technologically advanced optical character recognition machines in the world—machines that would effectively unplug the "data input bottleneck" (an all too-true phrase that was already gaining industry-wide popularity because it incisively summed-up the prevailing situation).

Philipson and his colleagues envisioned a cost-effective machine that could not only read data well, but would also be able to read a variety of type styles. They hoped to introduce a machine for the "Real World," a machine that would cope with data processing needs as they existed, without compelling machine users to standardize their input systems before reading equipment could be productive. They also sought to produce machines that could handle paper effectively and reliably move the kinds of paper most commonly found in information processing applications.

There were inevitable barriers that had to be dealt with before the Recognition machines could start making an impact in the commercial world. Such machines would not be easy to design or build, and the effort would require thousands of man-hours as well as thousands of dollars. Once built, the equipment would conceivably be difficult to market, since it would be costly and because the concept and uses of OCR in the business world were still relatively new and unproven over extended lengths of time.[16]

By early 1961, Herman Philipson was heavily involved in gathering the working capital necessary to establish his own independent OCR equipment manufacturing company. Speaking several years later to an audience composed of the directors of the Dallas Chamber of Commerce, Philipson recalled this early quest for financial backing:

"Being a Dallas native and having grown up in the Texas business climate, I was convinced that we could find initial financing, difficult as it would be, because then as now there is a spirit (in Texas) that allows people with good ideas to be given a chance."[17]

Evidently Philipson's perception of the local business attitudes was correct, since enough bankers in Texas (as well as elsewhere) agreed that the fledgling OCR company and its founder had demonstrated sufficient capabilities and had plans to merit their investment support. And so, Recognition Equipment was now in the business of building commercial OCR machines, competing against Farrington, IBM, and Control Data Corporation.

Then, like today, the minds and energies of the people of REI were its greatest assets. Philipson was the company's president; Gordon Perry was the "inventor"; Fred Davies was the administrator; and Jessica Eads and Barbara Smith offered secretarial support. These five were soon followed to REI by other "hedgehoppers," those former NDP employees who came to work for Recognition. (There was actually a knee-deep hedge between the two companies, hence the nickname.) Among the NDP emigrants were Len Nunley, whose field of greatest expertise was logic design, and Israel Sheinberg, whose responsibility at REI was electronics.

Sheinberg soon established a firm place of honor in the history of optical character recognition with the invention and development of the "Electronic Retina Computing Reader," which was announced by REI in 1962.[18] Sheinberg, like Philipson, was a native Texan, the son of a Fort Worth merchant. He had studied physics at the University of Texas and, later, worked as an electronics engineer for Hughes Aircraft in California. However, he returned to Texas to pursue the study of medicine at the Southwestern Medical School in Dallas. After a few semesters in medical school, Sheinberg discovered he was more interested in seeking answers to problems than in accepting medical diagnosis as unquestioned facts.[19] Therefore, "Is" Sheinberg returned to the engineering laboratory. As fate would have it, medical science's loss was one of OCR's most noteworthy gains.

Sheinberg's exposure to medicine and human anatomy, however, were not wasted. Working at the fledgling OCR company, he soon developed a light-sensing method based on the human eye and its natural, miraculous functionings. This device became known as the Electronic Retina, a key element in REI's outstandingly successful Electronic Retina Computing Reader (ERCR).

Like the retina of the human eye, the Electronic Retina added a new dimension to OCR technology. It compensated for imperfections in characters read by the system, ignoring smudges that would otherwise make the characters unreadable. It also "filled in" gray areas surrounding the characters. As Sheinberg said 15 years later, "We knew that if we could build a machine that could read as well as people do, we could sell it.

Throughout 1962 and 1963, the size of REI slowly increased. By mid-1962, the number of employees had more than doubled, and the company was building a machine shop behind the two-story company headquarters. REI celebrated its first anniversary with 35 employees. The company was making fast headway and needed additional space.

During those first few years, REI's engineering team applied their collective talents to more than optical character scanning. If their products were to be used successfully in the "Real World" of business, other technologies had to be effectively integrated into their systems. For example, paper-handling was almost as important to the equipment as the OCR components.

Since the company's products would be relatively expensive, the greatest market for potential buyers and users of REI equipment was among those prospective customers with large volumes of paper to handle and much of this paper would inevitably present handling problems: it would be dog-eared, stapled, torn, or otherwise abused. Airline companies with flimsy ticket copies, credit card-issuing companies, and banks with frequently handled receipts, and other similar institutions flooded with mountainous reams of imperfect paper, varying from tissue to card stock were all potential users of Recognition's OCR systems.

Through persistence, diligence and a seemingly unlimited supply of midnight oil, REI engineers progressively developed viable solutions to the paper-handling challenge. They developed mechanical features for their machines that provided comparatively fast throughput and simple maintenance. They also devised a reader that interfaced directly with a computer, and incorporated new electronics developments such as semiconductors into their equipment.[20]

In 1963, REI received five contracts, some of which were for non-OCR kinds of equipment. Among these contracts was one for a moon-landing simulator that was eventually sold to the National Aeronautics Space Administration (NASA).

Despite successful endeavors in only peripherally related technological areas, REI was by every standard an independent OCR company. By 1964, REI was ready to deliver its first optical scanning systems. In that year, the company installed the first ERCR in a commercial environment at the United Airlines offices in Chicago. This was the first ERCR to be used for reading airline tickets. Also in 1964, REI installed its first multifont reader, the Rapid Index Page Carrier (RIPC) at the Fireman's Fund Insurance Company in San Francisco.

By mid-1965, Recognition Equipment Incorporated employed over 300 employees and was occupying five buildings in central Dallas. The company and its OCR efforts visibly gained momentum. That year was one of many "firsts", as well as one significant last, for REI. The company opened its first regional office in Los Angeles, California. It also hired its first employee who would work outside of the United States, in Sweden, where one of the company's systems was installed at the Swedish Postal Bank ("POSTGIRO"). Additionally, 1965 was also the year in which REI's stock went public.

In that same year, REI installed the first OCR equipment for use in the printing and publications industry at Perry Publications. This ERCR installation marked the initial use of optical scanning for newspaper automation. Additionally in 1965, the first state government ordered an ERCR to apply OCR to motor vehicle registrations and drivers' license applications.

The year 1965 also marked Recognition's second and final incursion into the non-OCR field. The company built the moving ticker display board ("disk flipper") for the prestigious New York Stock Exchange. This disk flipper is still in daily use at the Stock Exchange.[21]

In early 1966, REI began construction on a new, much larger facility to encompass its expanding OCR equipment manufacturing operations and nearly 500 employees. In October of that same year, the company moved into new headquarters on Mockingbird Lane, in Dallas.

In the area of OCR product applications, 1966 was no less significant for REI. That year, Michigan became the second state government that used a Recognition ERCR to mechanize its "Master Driving Record Central Files" through the application of OCR equipment. In the first year of operation, this optical scanning system saved the State of Michigan over $200,000 and, during the first week of operation, identified 415 "unsafe" drivers.

Also in 1966, the first OCR system for the high-speed reading and sorting of credit card charge tickets and statements was ordered from REI by the American Express Company. That same year, Recognition installed the first operational multifont page reader (RIPC) for use by the Federal government at the U.S. Army Finance Center in Indianapolis. This RIPC was used to read allotment forms from American military installations throughout the world.

Interestingly enough, the forms read by The Finance Center's RIPC were prepared on virtually every kind of typewriter in existence, with no central control over the condition of these typewriters or the care exercised in the actual typing. During a 30-day period, this system read 63% of all of these heterogeneous documents error-free. The documents read contained both upper- and lower-case letters from more than 30 different fonts.

In the milestone OCR-use year of 1966, Recognition also announced equipment which had the capability of reading the full alpha-numeric handprint set through the employment of optical scanning. In this application, handprint was intermixed with typed or printed information on the same document.[22]

In 1967, the ink-jet printer (IJP), developed by REI for use in its OCR systems, was selected one of the most "Significant Technological Products" introduced in American industry during the year. That same year, the company installed the first integrated OCR/IJP equipment for use in an oil company with the delivery of several ERCR IJP systems to Texaco in Houston. These systems were used for credit card document processing.

The commercial OCR business was booming at REI in Texas. In March of 1967, the company welcomed its 500th employee. Scarcely 16 months later, in July of 1968, the 1000th employee walked through the doors. The company's seventh anniversary, November 2, 1968, was celebrated by 1,250 employees and, at about the same time, REI established another international subsidiary. This one was in Japan.

In 1968, REI announced its "Remote Time-Sharing Retina." The technology associated with this vital development allowed hundreds of terminal devices employing Remote Time-Sharing Retinas to be connected to a central recognition unit. This innovation represents a direct antecedant to today's decentralized OCR data entry systems which are used in distributed data entry networks.[23]

The year 1968 was also noteworthy for REI. In that year, the company delivered its first high-speed OCR document transports to several oil companies. These transports moved paper at a blinding rate of speed, 2400 documents per minute.[24]

In 1969, the company shipped its first high-speed multi-font OCR system to the United States Post Office. Interest in the many possible applications of OCR for achieving better mail service had not diminished.

In the same year, Philipson's company was again honored. This time REI was named the Dallas "Exporter of the Year" by the Dallas Market Center "for having achieved the most significant progress in developing world trade with Dallas.'' To mark its eighth anniversary, plans were announced to move REI's 1726 employees to yet another site. A 200,000-square foot plant was to be built in Irving, Texas across from the Texas Stadium, home of the National Football League's Dallas Cowboys. Today, the company is still headquartered on this site.

Chapter Five

Sales, Service, and Standardization

As might easily be imagined, OCR's progress during the 1960's was not confined solely to the new developments and commercial achievements attributed to Recognition Equipment. The dedication to OCR research, engineering and marketing had never flagged in the many other companies which had been, to varying degrees, actively involved in some form of optical scanning for a decade or more before REI was conceived in Herman Philipson's imagination. And, understandably, as OCR's prospects and potential profitability became even more apparent throughout the data processing world, new companies were founded to join in the business of manufacturing and marketing optical scanning equipment.

Some of these new OCR-oriented companies of the 1960's, like REI, possessed enough energy, innovation, technical expertise and financial resources to attain various measures of success, and are still in business. More, however, fell by the wayside and either changed their technological and/or marketing directions or are no longer in operation.

According to an article published in "Data Processing Magazine" in mid-1970, five companies were engaged in the active development and/or marketing of OCR readers in 1967: Farrington, IBM, Control Data, Optical Scanning Corporation and Recognition Equipment. RCA, Philco and NCR were also marketing specialized reading machines, but were not "fully" in the OCR field.

This same article went on to cite four general groups of OCR readers, classified by type of input, which were in use by 1966. These were page readers, which read 8 ½-by-11 inch documents; document readers, which read a line or two from small documents (2-by-4 to 4-by-8 inches); journal tape readers, which read printed cash register or adding machine listing tapes; and reader-punches, which read data printed on tab cards and punched this data into the same cards, similar to interpreters in reverse.

This interesting 1970 magazine perspective on the OCR field also stated that page readers tended to be large, expensive, multifont machines because of the flexibility required to scan the loose formats of varying pages and because the large sized medium required delicate movements of either the optical system itself or the paper handling system to scan large data areas. Document readers, journal tape readers and reader punches, however, fared somewhat better in that particular writer's judgement because, even when these were multifont machines, they were less expensive since they featured less complex transports and smaller scanning areas were required for their types of input.[25]

Throughout the decade, many significant new technological developments were offered to businesses and various government entities by the various OCR vendor companies. While it is impossible within the scope of this history to mention all of these noteworthy companies and to list all of their important sales during this era, a general overview of selected events and developments follows to provide a reasonable perspective of the OCR industry during the 1960's.

Control Data Corporation's early commercial optical scanning machine was the model "915 Page Reader." The first CDC 915 was installed at the Crocker Citizens National Bank in San Francisco in October, 1965. Three years later, in October, 1968, Control Data announced the model 935 document carrier, which also made use of a columnar scanner for capturing characters read by OCR for transaction-processing applications.[26] Control Data Corporation, as stated earlier, was at this time fully utilizing the considerable technological expertise of Dr. Jacob Rabinow and his colleagues in the development of its OCR products.

In a 1969 "Datamation" article provocatively entitled, "Whither OCR?", Dr. Rabinow discussed some OCR endeavors and especially those of Control Data. "If one wants to read pages with OCR at fairly high speeds", he wrote "one should expect to spend from one-half to two million dollars, and the speed will be something between 500 and 14,000 characters per second. At the top of this scale stands the Bank of America machine developed by Control Data Corporation that reads seven different styles of printing at the interesting rate of 14,000 characters per second. Then there is the IBM 1975 built for the Social Security Administration which reads a wide variety of fonts and for which the price is not known. There are also multifont machines built by Recognition Equipment, Philco-Ford, Scan Data and others."

Rabinow continued, "Moving down the price scale, one comes to more limited machines which may be either of the page-reading or document-reading variety. Such machines are built by many manufacturers, and the prices vary from perhaps $50,000 to $500,000, depending on the flexibility of control, the number of fonts, the number of output sorts, etc."

"Finally", he stated, "there are just beginning to appear low-priced machines for limited applications. One approach is to locate only a remote scanner mechanism on the premises of the user. This scanning device converts the visual image of the paper into an electrical signal and transmit video signals over telephone wires to the recognition machine proper, (which is) operated at some central location. Cognitronics Company, under the direction of Dave Shepard, has built and demonstrated such equipment. A remote scanner system has also been announced by Recognition Equipment."

Rabinow added, "Other workers in the field, including my group at Control Data, have played with this approach, and it does seem to have particular promise in applications where the permissible speed can be low, the amount of data small, and the character shapes difficult to analyze by simple equipment. Another approach to low-cost readers is that taken by us at Control Data, where we have built and demonstrated several machines designed to read one line on a document at low speed and using a controlled font such as USASI-A (i.e. OCR "A"). Such machines can be sold for something like $5000 and up."[27]

The 1960's proved to be a fruitful decade for companies other than Control Data. IBM, one of the veteran OCR reading machine makers, was in no way content to rest on its laurels after the delivery of its high-speed multifont reader, the IBM "1975", to the Federal government for use at the Social Security Administration in 1965. This vast and vigorous company would follow-up during the next few years with other OCR-based types of equipment.

Notable among these IBM machines were the "1287" document reader and the "1288" page reader, which were introduced in 1968. Both of these OCR products were installed on-line for interface with the company's "360" line of computer systems. Models of these devices variously read several fonts and documents of many differing sizes.

Cognitronics, the company founded by Dr. David Shepherd after leaving Farrington, offered the first remote OCR service to users in 1969. As mentioned by Dr. Rabinow, this relatively early form of OCR was used for distributed data entry and enabled users to input transactions through the application of optical readers at their sites for subsequent processing at a remote central computer.

Cognitronics maintained an OCR service bureau in order to bring this remote application of optical scanning to customers. The service bureau employed remote facsimile transmission terminals and either magnetic tape terminals on the users' premises or a delivery service for output tapes recorded at the service center. This Cognitronics service was leased for as little as $725 per month. Cost varied with volume, format, font and type quality of the input data, and distance from the user's location to the service center.[28]

In the late 1960's, Scan-Data, CompuScan and Information International produced readers capable of reading large numbers of fonts and sizes. In addition, these readers mixed fonts sizes on a page and read both fixed and proportional spacing.

Scan-Data introduced OCR devices for the graphics industry and produced three models of equipment: specifically, the "100" and "300" Readers, which read up to 50 fonts each and the "200" which read from one to five fonts. The "100" was aimed specifically at graphics applications, while the "300" was primarily for use in the business environment.

The flexibility and versatility of these Scan-Data OCR systems were the direct result of extensive software control of the optical scanning components and the handwired features used in recognition, together with a "double correlation" recognition technique that would first define small features comprising characters and then total character identity on the basis of a percentage of probability. Monthly rentals for these Scan-Data machines began at $700, while the larger Scan-Data "100" and "300" models were priced at approximately $325,000.

At about the same time Scan-Data was introducing readers, CompuScan announced the first commercially marketed omnifont reader, one capable of reading virtually any font. This was the CompuScan "370" image processor, a processor capable of accommodating both graphic images and alphanumeric fonts.

Two "370" prototype models were installed at a service bureau in New Jersey. The "370" used software almost exclusively in recognition logic to obtain the comparatively "astounding" flexibility of recognizing any font's characters. New fonts were "learned" simply by being read in from microfilm and then identified character-by-character via a CRT terminal keyboard. The learning process took approximately ten minutes, and sometimes included filling in degraded characters with a light pen so that the resulting reference masks in the system's memory would come as close as possible to being ideal. CompuScan planned to deliver working models of their omnifont readers by late 1970 at a cost of about $900,000 each.[30]

Recognition capabilities based upon software was the main feature of Information International's "Graphics I" reader. The "Graphics I" was an omnifont reader with many of the same characteristics of CompuScan's "370", including image processing capabilities of all kinds, the use of microfilm as an input medium, and the ability to adopt new fonts read in through the use of a CRT terminal.

CompuScan's "370" and Information International's "Graphics I" were memorable not only for their omnifont capabilities, but also because these machines were the early examples of equipment using microfilm as the input medium for a page reader. However, because microfilming was utilized as an intermediary process for these readers, rather than as their primary input medium, the equipment was promoted as page readers rather than microfilm units.[31]

In the mid to late 1960's, other companies also competed enthusiastically in the commercial OCR field. Journal tape readers were produced by NCR and Farrington, but most OCR equipment manufacturers dealt with journal tape processing needs by offering additional journal tape feed options to their readers which were designed basically for other types of input.[32]

During the decade, Addressograph—Multigraph developed a bar-code reader. Optical Scanning Corporation introduced optical mark readers and Datatype developed its own type of low-cost optical readers that used specially typed bar codes.[33]

Data Recognition of California also developed limited capability OCR equipment. The "DRC 700" read account numbers from documents the size of 51- and 80- column tab cards imprinted by bank credit cards. The device was, in reality, an intermediary reader-printer. This West Coast company was established specifically to develop new types of low-cost OCR devices directed to precisely defined applications based on detailed studies of the needs of the perceived markets.

Turnaround billing applications were long considered the "bread and butter" of the commercial OCR industry. Univac's "2703 Document Reader" was a prime example of employing this capability as an OCR marketing strategy. The Univac "2703" was primarily designed and used for turnaround billing and was limited to reading numerical data and one or two lines of print from a specific location. Typical applications of the "2703" were utility bills which offered the close tolerances necessary for this particular document reader.[34]

The above examples serve as illustrations of the emergence of new and important OCR technological advances, applications and sales that were prevalent during the 1960's. The list, though not complete, does effectively illustrate just how far optical scanning had progressed in a mere ten years.

With the apparent proliferation of OCR devices, the necessity for establishing font standardization became more pressing than ever before. Jacob Rabinow, historically an outspoken advocate of greater standardization, put forward the case for standardization most convincingly when he wrote, in 1969, "The more control one puts into a document, the simpler and less costly is the reading machine . . . Now how can we get this control? The answer is 'Standardize'. Standardize the type of paper, standardize the size of the paper, standardize the quality of printing, standardize the format, and standardize the font."[35] Rabinow was, of course, joined by many other OCR standardization advocates, who came forward from the various optical scanning equipment users and manufacturers.

Finally, in 1966, the American National Standards Institute, Committee X3A working under the sponsorship of the Business Equipment Manufacturers Association (BEMA), completed a thorough study of OCR requirements and adopted a standard character set, the "USASI-A" font, which is commonly referred to as

"OCR-A". This font, while not completely satisfying all parties involved in the selection process, was generally accepted by the users and manufacturers of optical scanning equipment in the United States.

The highly stylized OCR-A font was designed to facilitate optical recognition and, therefore substantially differs in appearance from most typewriter fonts. However, OCR-A can be read by human eyes even though they will not read it as easily as other non-stylized fonts.

The original 1966 USASI set of characters included uppercase alphabetics, numerics and 33 different representative symbols (dollar signs, punctuation, etc.). By 1969, standards for lowercase characters were added to the OCR-A and font standardization for OCR use was virtually complete, for use in America. The entire standard was identified as USAS1 X3.17-1966.

European OCR systems manufacturers and users had somewhat different ideas about how machine fonts should look. Moreover, they were as vehement as their U.S.A. counterparts in recognizing and stating the need for OCR standardization.

The Europeans, therefore, designed their own font to be used with optical scanning devices. This European font was officially called "ISO-B" and later became commonly known as OCR-B. While OCR-B was in the opinion of many manufacturers and users more "aesthetically" pleasing than OCR-A, the European font initially presented some problems to the majority of OCR equipment makers, especially the Americans.[36] Eventually in the 1960's, most optical scanning systems were engineered to accommodate the European font as well as the American one. The net result of font standardization on both sides of the Atlantic far outweighed the drawbacks caused by their differences.

As the 1960's drew to a close, OCR was in a strong position as a specialized area of the data processing industry and was largely viewed as a major breakthrough which could solve the "input bottleneck" that threatened to slow down the progress made in second generation computers. First generation OCR scanners had been in operation for a number of years and, according to one estimate made early in 1968, 400 to 500 OCR readers were in use in the United States alone.

At about the same point in time, several Chicago area companies installing or evaluating second generation OCR systems gravitated towards each other to exchange experiences and explore new ideas for optical scanning applications. These meetings resulted in some very meaningful accomplishments, including systems, software ideas, OCR problem solutions and experiences with paper, forms, and image capturing devices. The effective exchange of such ideas gave rise to other, even more exciting questions: "What if a national group of users of optical scanning equipment could assemble someplace to learn from each others' experiences? Wouldn't it be highly beneficial to form our own organization?"

To answer these questions a two-day meeting was held in Houston, Texas in June, 1970. At that meeting, the OCR Users Association became a reality.

Chapter Six

"Why Should I Use OCR?"

At the onset of the seventies, the state of the art for OCR technology and applications had progressed to a point where reasons for using OCR became readily apparent. Over the years, as OCR technology evolved, the manufacturers of optical scanning equipment and systems consistently concentrated their efforts on providing system solutions which enabled users to reduce and control data entry costs while simultaneously improving information quality.

Mature OCR technologies have significantly reduced the time and expense required for data entry while, at the same time, providing increased control. The inherent flexibilities of OCR's proven data entry systems readily permitted system upgrading as the users' applications evolved, while minimizing the impact to the users' production schedules and operating costs. By addressing data entry at its source, OCR equipment now possessed the capability of reading real-world and field-prepared source documents and bypassing the highly labor-intensive key entry function. Furthermore, since the mid-1960's, OCR manufacturers developed important product strengths and proven system capabilities which encompassed a number of key technologies allowing for many cost-effective increases in productivity.

The first and most relevant of these technologies was optical character recognition itself, including the ability of OCR equipment to readily read even badly degraded ''real-world'' characters at high speeds. (''Real-world'' is a key phrase in this history. The fact that OCR systems can rapidly read the same degraded printed characters read by people elevates optical scanning's potential far above that of other, competitive data entry technologies.)

The second key technology was the capability of OCR equipment to handle real-world paper quickly and reliably. This paper ranges from flimsy, carbon-backed airline tickets to heavy letter mail, and from credit card receipts to cents-off coupons crudely clipped or ripped from the backs of cereal boxes. Additionally, scanning equipment was capable of effectively handling, on an intermixed basis, a wide variety of documents of different sizes and weights, and documents which may be folded, spindled or bent. This ''milieu'' represents source data's ''real world.''

A third major technology was that of systems and software integration. OCR equipment had the capability of integrating complex, multiple processors into highly efficient systems that include large-scale computers communicating interactively with mini- and micro-processors.

The fourth major technology was that of non-impact printing. Using this technology, the equipment printed human-readable characters or ''intelligent'' bars on documents that represented data that had been read by means of optical scanning, thus providing what might be called an ''escort memory.'' This attribute was generated by the projection of minute droplets of ink directly on the paper in a predetermined pattern under the program control of the OCR system while the paper was in the transport and was in motion. This process was accomplished without decreasing the speed of the paper throughput in the system.[37]

The technology (-ies) of OCR had been adapted and applied liberally to a diverse variety of data entry and data manipulation tasks. For example, OCR has been applied (either in the decades already discussed or in those yet to be discussed) for reading typewritten manuscript copy and converting the resultant data to magnetic media format for storage, typesetting or text editing; for the reading and sorting of letter mail; for the reading and sorting of Federal currency and consumer clipped coupons; for the reading and processing of payment remittance items such as utility, credit card, installment or premium payments; for the reading of printed material and the conversion of the text into some form of audible narration (primarily for the blind); for the partial or total control of check processing for banks; for the reading and processing of adding machine journal tapes; and, for the control of various retail store operations by reading product codes at the point-of-sale or in inventory environments.

By the late 1970's, OCR had, in fact, been applied, with varying measures of success, to virtually every area of data entry. Of course, the basic foundation for employing optical scanning systems has always been, and will probably always be, economic justification—cost-effectiveness and measurably increased productivity for the users. OCR will most assuredly proliferate as long as methods of accomplishing data entry are cheaper, faster and/or more accurate than alternative data entry techniques.

What, then, were some of these alternative forms of data entry techniques? The four major forms are punched cards, key-to-tape, key-to-disk and video terminal key entry techniques. "Keying" in some form is an integral aspect of each of these methods of data entry.

OCR's "edge" over each of these more labor-intensive alternatives becomes quickly apparent. When used properly, OCR eliminates the comparatively expensive human labor required to transform data from "source documents" into computer-useable format. In general, when an optical scanner "reads" the data on a form, a data-keying operation by a person is not required or becomes secondary (for reject reentry).

However, the OCR system's ability to operate is highly dependent on the preparation of the source documents to be read within scannable format perimeters. The data have to be appropriately printed, imprinted, typed or hand-printed to meet the specific OCR equipment's requirements and scope of reading capabilities. And, to paraphrase the Bard of Avon, "Aye, there's the rub," which may be accurately attributed with playing a leading role in holding back OCR from becoming our current, standard data entry mode. The enormous data entry requirements and emergent computer capabilities of the past three decades quite literally surpassed the various standardizations required to bring OCR's potential to full and widespread fruition.

By the time OCR technology had been developed to the point of being both dependable and cost-effective, the "Hollerith" punch card had become established as the standard form of data entry. Punched cards, although requiring a relatively great amount of labor-intensiveness, represented to users and potential users an easily-understood, established data entry mode. (The De Facto Standard).

The late development of OCR standards measurably restrained both the growth and use of optical character recognition in all phases of business, as well in other potential OCR markets. The infinite number of character and mark patterns and document sizes, shapes and weights, when compared with the preciseness and rigorous characteristics of punched cards, for a long time exerted a negative influence upon the acceptance of OCR as a "standard" data entry technique.

Other factors also played a part in impeding OCR's progress during the 1960's and 1970's. Chief among these was the cost of most optical scanning systems versus the cost for data entry via key devices. OCR batch processors, in particular, have always required greater capital outlays by customers than keying equipment and there was inevitably a minimum data entry volume level below which OCR may not have been the best economic solution to a user's specific needs.

Despite these and other perceived drawbacks, OCR as a viable effective data entry technique has proven itself, both from a marketing and a technological standpoint. A great variety of OCR systems of many shapes, sizes, forms and capabilities were available to users. Both custom-made and standardized OCR systems were are now available and being used in impressive quantities.

In the late 70's, optical character recognition systems could generally be classified into one or more of three basic types: character readers, which can scan alphanumeric text and, combining hardware and software, logically determine which characters are being scanned; bar code readers, which are designed to be used with black lines and bars representing characters when put into specific combinations; and optical mark readers, which scan for the presence or absence of black marks in predefined locations. These three forms of OCR represented nearly the total scope of the commercial applications of optical scanning technology, with the character readers representing OCR's major technological accomplishment. More specific applications involving some form of OCR technology were also used for such applications as photographic terrain analysis and graphic reproduction—but these "esoteric" applications had only a minimal bearing on OCR's evolution and application in information processing.

Most basic optical character recognition systems were comprised of three major functional sections: the detection section, the recognition section and the output section. In addition, a transport mechanism was usually a component when the transport or movement of the paper was required.

The detection component of the system was responsible for "seeing" a particular black pattern on a document and determining whether that pattern was a "character", a "mark", or a "bar code". This component does not attempt to interpret the pattern as being a particular character. It simply detects the presence of a pattern. The detection component is composed of a electro-optical hardware system which was able to differentiate white from black or even intermediate shades of gray. Several alternative techniques existed which performed the detection function. However, the objective of each technological capability remained the same for all; the "Data Lifting" function.

The responsibility for interpreting a particular pattern as a specific character belonged to the recognition portion of the system. Recognition may be achieved in various ways. In some systems, recognition was primarily a hardware function while in others, software was used to analyze and discriminate the "meaning" of a detected pattern.

Each OCR system had at least one method of "outputting" recognized data values. There are two main categories of output: 1) On-line Output—OCR stystems are on-line if they send recognized data directly to a processing device (such as a computer) which uses the data immediately to perform some processing function: and 2) Stored Output—Most OCR systems stored recognized data on standard computer magnetic tape. This data then became available for what was called "off-line application processing." That is, the data which was read and could be used by the user at his convenience.

Output from OCR devices took many additional forms. For example, OCR devices have been designed to assist the blind. These devices will scan printed text and convert that text into output which is audible narration. Different types of OCR devices are often used to enter draft-typewritten materials into a word processing system or to convert draft-typewritten materials into typeset material. This saves the time and labor of re-keying text material. In fact, the output section of optical scanners can and had been adapted to interface with virtually any device that can accept formatted output data.

Finally, documents are moved through an optical reader by means of the transport, a very critical element in a total optical scanning system. Transports have been designed to reliably carry paper documents of widely ranging sizes, weights and shapes. The speed and reliability of the transport relate directly to the throughput efficiency of any particular system. In the development of OCR equipment, an enormous amount of energy and expense has been expended in the development for fast, error-free transports.

There are, incidentally, a number of OCR devices which do not require a paper transport. This situation usually occurs in one of two ways. The detection unit may be small and portable enough to be moved by hand across the document to be read (i.e., an OCR wand). On the other hand, if the detection scanner is stationary, the item to be read can be moved by hand across the scanning area. In either case, a transport mechanism is unnecessary.

Relevant to this technological discussion, are the techniques and tools that manufacturers have been using to build optical devices. Those advances beneficial to electronics over the past 20 years have, in general, affected the OCR business. Innovations such as transistors, printed circuit technology, digital memory improvements, television technology, photocell developments, lasers and other electronic and electro-optical techniques have made a major impact upon the OCR business.

Manufacturers of OCR equipments have used these techniques in various ways to increase speed, accuracy and overall reliability of the systems supplied to the users. The manufacturer's choice of detection and recognition system used in building any specific optical reader depended upon many factors. Included among these factors were the types of fonts to be read, the desired price of the OCR equipment, speed constraints and considerations, and the precision of the discrimination required.

Most of the modern techniques applied to detection scanning provided satisfactory results as long as the capability of the total system design matched the requirements of the users applications. Therefore, an OCR system would not be selected merely because a particular scanning technique is used, but rather because of its ability to perform one or a number of specific application tasks more effectively.

For example, detection scanning components have been built around mechanical rotating disks, controlled cathode ray tube beams (i.e., "flying spot"), column-arranged photocells, vidicon tubes, laser beams, and light-emitting diodes. Each of these detection scanning modes offers certain advantages in terms of price, efficiency and accuracy where they are used to detect particular types of patterns. However, a true test of system performance can be made only when the detection component is combined with the recognition components. In this way, performance on documents and data of the type that will be processed by a particular application can be read and measured for both speed and accuracy. Although no attempt to explain or compare the various scanning techniques used to detect patterns, will be made here, it is important to note that the bulk of these scanning techniques were developed in the two decades from 1950 through 1970, and have been applied successfully in a significant number of data processing applications.

The recognition portion of the OCR system is perhaps of greater interest to a potential user of OCR because the output directly affects the application being processed. In other words, the way characters are recognized directly affects the recognition rates, rejection rates and substitution rates that occur with any scanning system. These concepts are crucial to understanding optical recognition and there is, consequently, one "given" axiom in optical recognition which is absolutely true of almost any OCR system: more specifically, the rate of correct character recognition is directly proportional to the quality of source data. If a character is perfectly formed and printed, most OCR systems will nearly always have the capability of correctly recognizing that character.

When recognition problems occur, such problems are primarily due to trying to read imperfect characters. These imperfections will realistically occur in almost any application, but they are more prevalent in some such as credit cards and turn around documents. They most frequently result because no printing system is perfect. For example, bad ribbons, bent keys, misaligned carriages and platens can all cause imperfect typewritten characters. Imprinters (such as those devices used in the processing of credit card numbers on receipts), high speed printers and even offset printing can also produce smudged or imperfect characters. Additionally, handprinted characters are subject to all of the conceivable variables that human beings make.

If there is any one area that attracted the attention of OCR equipment manufacturers, it was the development of recognition and discrimination techniques which allow a high level of recognition of less-than-perfectly formed characters. The record on this particular OCR has been a good one. As a result of developments made during the fiercely competitive OCR marketplace of the 1960's, modern systems reflect a high performance record even with data that is very difficult to read. Consequently, the history of OCR applications indicates, that rejected data is not a serious problem. A data character may be defined as being rejected by an OCR system when the recognition unit cannot determine the value of the pattern. When this occurs, the OCR system generally indicates to the system's user that a particular document contains a rejected character. Several alternative methods are then used to determine the character and input the desired data value to the system.

More serious, however, is the problem of substitution. Substitution occurs when a data character is incorrectly read and accepted by the OCR system as something other than what was originally intended. Substitution, then, can become a problem since an error has occurred but no error indication has been communicated. Generally, for most applications, a reasonable level of rejection is both expected and tolerable; but substitution must be held to a minimum.

In the more labor-intensive data entry modes, such as those involving keying operations, almost all errors made are substitution errors. An operator who keys an incorrect character is, in fact, making a substitution error. Therefore, OCR systems are subject to the same type of errors that are commonly made by manual key entry. The basic requirement for users of OCR devices is to provide the highest quality input data possible. This simple procedure ensures that substitution levels are well within tolerable limits.

Any OCR system will perform only as well as the support received from its users. In many cases, systems with minimally controlled data production provide an enormous return on investment in data entry labor savings.

Even though this aspect of OCR is within the realm of the system user's control, manufacturers have progressively designed recognition units capable of very sophisticated and effective recognition processes. Most of the recognition techniques used in OCR systems fall into one of the following two categories:

The first of these recognition techniques is one in which the matrix of character signals generated by the scanner is matched against a reference matrix representative of what should be obtained for a particular character. Each of these matrices is, in effect, a template or character model. The accuracy of the resulting match is then used to determine which character best fits the scanned character.

The other recognition technique is called "feature analysis." There are many variations of feature or stroke analysis, however, they all rely on matching certain elements of a scanned character with typical reference elements for each character stored in the systems font memory. Typically, the scanned elements for each character are sent through a logic discrimination sequence which attempts to determine the correct character match.

These descriptions of two recognition processes used in optical scanning devices represent simplified explanations for each classification. In reality, many variations of these techniques, employing any number of hardware and software techniques, have been applied to optical character recognition.

Character recognition technology is a very exacting process and is by no means perfect. "Trade-offs" must be resolved by each user in terms of the criteria allowed for accepting or rejecting characters. In brief, character recognition is a combination of scanning accuracy and discrimination, recognition logic and discrimination techniques, and established acceptance criteria that will determine the performance characteristics of any specific scanner.

In order to determine the overall performance of an OCR system, consideration must be given to such closely associated issues as speed of operation, transport considerations, data correction features and specific application characteristics including document design and font selection. The variety of OCR devices available then was adequate to provide and economic benefit to most users of applications with sufficient volume.

Chapter Seven

A Mature Technology: 1970-80

Optical character recognition had come a long way by 1970. In that year alone, the estimated value of OCR equipment shipped by manufacturers to users totalled approximately $150 million.

OCR had emphatically asserted itself as a technology which held "great expectations" in the commercial and government market place. Similar to the growth phases experienced by humans, optical scanning had passed through various chronologically identifiable periods of evolution: conception, infancy, puberty, and adolescence. By 1970, a youthful OCR was embarking upon "young adulthood" and was quickly maturing toward a productive technology.

Within the decade of the seventies, many systems achievements and improvements were logged. Many companies were involved in the manufacture and marketing of systems. Many new OCR equipment manufacturers were entering (and, occasionally, departing) the optical scanning scene. (Some appreciation for the range of this activity may be gained from appendix "B", an OCR chronology.) Attempting to describe each individual and noteworthy OCR development that occurred during the decade would be parallel attempting to detail the accomplishments and applications of every computer manufacturer and user during the 1970s. For this reason, a comprehensive OCR development chronology is beyond the scope of this history. Therefore, to provide a concise general overview of OCR's business growth and applications from 1970 to 1980 and to offer some perspective into this dynamic decade of optical scannings' expansion, this chapter focuses on two selected aspects of the total OCR industry during this ten-year span.

First the July, 1977 conference of the Optical Character Recognition Users Association (OCRUA) is discussed. This conference, held in Washington, D.C., was especially significant because it represented the largest OCRUA meeting to date and because it offered the data processing world a more detailed and comprehensive overview of OCR's contemporary status than had ever been realized. After reviewing this conference, the steady growth, systems achievements, and installation of OCR equipment that took place throughout the 1970s is presented.

The July, 1977 OCRUA conference attracted over 300 optical scanning equipment manufacturers, users and other interested individuals from around the United States and from several foreign nations. However, as reported in a "Data Entry Awareness Report" entitled, "OCR Revisited" published soon thereafter, "the conference attendance figures should have been in the thousands, because it offered the data processing technology (field) the most detailed analysis of this data entry technology for years. It combined both an excellent display of operating OCR systems with well thought-out program sessions."

The conference report detailed how OCR systems marketing and usage had "begun to take a new turn" during the 1970s. The report brought out that OCR had almost been "completely forgotten" in the late 1960s when keyboard-to-tape and keyboard-to-disc data entry equipment had been introduced along with CRT and intelligent terminals. This report also went on to state that instead of competing against key entry systems, OCR was now "joining" them with the resulting mixed media and application - oriented system(s) making both the optical data entry and keyboard data entry concepts "stronger, allowing each to be employed in its most effective way."

The theme of this 1977 conference was "The Economics of OCR" and strong emphasis throughout the meetings was placed on optical scanning's specific applications in various areas of business and industry. Technological aspects were only peripherally touched upon, indicating that the reliability of OCR equipment readers was no longer a major concern. As stated in the previously mentioned Data Entry Awareness Report, "Attendees felt confident the (OCR) systems could do the job."

Remittance-processing OCR applications seemed to attract the greatest part of the conference's attention. Ten conference discussion sessions dealt with remittance processing either directly or indirectly. Six of the conference equipment vendors simply referred to their scanning systems as "types of payment or remittance-processing OCR systems."

The general interest in OCR's present and future was, perhaps, best reflected at the four well attended education sessions, where optical scanning's current status was discussed at length. The points covered at these specific sessions came closest to "hitting the bulls' eye" of the audience's needs and reasons for attending this conference.

Among the many varied OCR products exhibited and/or demonstrated were several types of systems brought in by those companies exclusively dedicated to the development of OCR technology and equipment and, in addition, by those only marginally involved in the optical scanning business environment. Some of the exhibitors represented well-known and widely respected multinational conglomerates; others were relatively small companies known only in their local areas of operation. This mixture of types of exhibitors was especially interesting and reflected the resurgence of interest in OCR which occurred during the latter part of the 1970s.

This OCRUA conference afforded all attendees a rare opportunity to see many different types and sizes of OCR equipment in one compact area. The exhibits represented a wide, although not complete range of OCR applications and the prices of products shown covered a broad spectrum. Some of the eager users even brought their own business forms in order to test the various equipment's scanning capabilities on-the-spot.

In addition to reviewing the types of seminars and other learning sessions offered at this OCRUA conference and, perhaps, even more indicative of the far-reaching progress-to-date of OCR than the types of equipment displayed, is delving into the "generic" composition of the more than 300 persons who attended this important meeting. Approximately one-half of the total attendance was composed of idividuals who were "new" to the OCR field. These persons were interested in finding out more about how future technology could benefit their specific companies and agencies.

Furthermore, OCR interested parties from outside of the United States travelled to Washington to attend this conference. Representatives of Europe's OCR Association (EUROCRA) were there. At this conference, Eric Lundberg, head of EUROCRA, estimated that his organization had about 200 members representing 12 different European nations and that there were nearly 800 OCR equipment users on the European continent.

The Washington conference was composed of a productive, mixture of OCR vendors, users, technologists and business persons. By nearly every standard, the conference was a success and demonstrated categorically to the data processing industry that optical scanning was continuing its forward progress as a viable, attractive, cost-effective means for data entry. The 1977 summer meeting set the pace for a series of semi-annual meetings and summer equipment and supply expositions for attendees and suppliers.

Within the OCR business world, by late 1970, a number of companies and corporations were gearing up to meet the growing market for optical character readers. These included REI, IBM, Scan-Data, Cognitronics, Scan Optics, Control Data, NCR, Burroughs, and a number of others which were soon to follow. Paper and forms suppliers such as UARCO, Moore, and Standard Register made special provisions to meet and improve design standards and specifications which would greatly improve throughput and read rates. The stage was set for the decade of dynamic growth which was to follow.

A corporate front runner at that time was REI which had just completed and occupied its new, 200,000 square foot facilities in Irving, Texas, and had announced four important new optical scanning products. These new systems were the "Input 80", "Input 3", "Input Image", and "Output Image".

Most noteworthy of the new systems was the Input 80, a highly versatile but expensive page reader. Presently, this system continues, in its most recent variations, to be one of the most successful OCR products ever developed. The original Input 80 used an "Integrated Retina", which was an integrated circuit reading device with 96 photodiodes incorporated into a single slice of silicon only 1.5 inches in length. This extensive application of integrated circuitry eliminated the need for hundreds of semiconductors and miscellaneous connections.

Like the Electronic Retina, the Integrated Retina was modeled after the functionings of the human eye, compensating for imperfections in the material read. However, the Integrated Retina additionally normalized or made adjustments for size variations, thereby permitting far more flexible reading assignments. Furthermore, at the speed of 3,600 characters per second, the Integrated Retina possessed much faster speed capabilities than the Electronic Retina.

The Input 80 system that used the Integrated Retina accurately read information from full-size sheets of paper at speeds in excess of 2,200 pages per hour, or the equivalent of more than 500 hours of keypunching. Therefore, through the use of the Input 80 and its Integrated Retina, REI was achieving one critical business goal: the company was offering the data processing industry a form of data entry system that enabled customers to meet their data entry needs at lower costs than previously available. The result was noticeably greater OCR user productivity.

The company's Input 3 system was designed as the primary

means of data entry for IBM's "System 3" computers. The Input 3 was directly connectable to both the IBM "360" and "370" computers, but could also be used in "stand-alone" working environments.

In 1970, Recognition announced the receipt of a $7 million contract from the United States Postal Service for the development of an advanced optical character recognition system. According to postal officials, this contract represented the first major commitment by the Postal Service to automate the handling of America's mail.

This important contract, called for the development of a system that could process up to 86,000 letter-size pieces of mail per hour and set the tone for REI's many domestic postal activities later in the decade. This OCR reader was to have the capability of finding an address located at various places on an envelope face and of reading accurately through address windows. The system would also disregard extraneous information.

Through a technique of context analysis, the USPS system built by Recognition would also possess the capability of correctly identifying addresses which contained misspelled words. For example, if an address contained the word "Chicalo" instead of "Chicago", the system would make the appropriate destination identification and forward the letter to the intended city.

Despite the company's new products and such major contracts as the one from the U.S. Postal Service, 1970 proved to be the most difficult business year yet experienced by REI. Because of the prevailing recessionary atmosphere, the company's employment figure had to be reduced by several hundred and REI reported a substantial net loss for the fiscal year. In a related development, that same year, Recognition sold Docutel, one of its domestic subsidiaries, which had been formed earlier.

Unlike some of the other OCR companies, REI weathered the economic pressures of 1970 and continued to maintain its leadership in the optical scanning business throughout the seventies. At the end of fiscal 1971, Recognition once again announced a profit. This was a sharp reversal of its disappointing 1970 financial statistics. That same year, the company announced the receipt of its first postal contract for OCR equipment to be used outside the United States. By the end of fiscal 1972, the company concluded yearly operations with the highest backlog figure ever registered by REI. This key indicator of the company's health was primarily attributed to the success of the INPUT 80 in United States, the European postal systems, and Recognition's entry into the enormous North American check processing market with the sale of the first TRACE system.

The TRACE system represented a significant technological step forward from its direct antecedent, the Electronic Retina Computing Reader (ERCR). The name "TRACE" was the acronym for "Transaction Control and Encoding" system. Using advanced OCR technology, the TRACE system read and processed up to 2,000 checks per minute, and, in some credit card applications, the rate climbed to 2,400 items per minute.

While the TRACE system was an example of technological achievement, its greatest asset was the ability to provide effective solutions to many financial industry customers' most "cost-sensitive" problems. Traditionally, banks had filed checks by hand, in huge "tub files" until the day in each monthly cycle when they were sorted and returned to their customers. This repetitive, labor-intensive sorting and handling was a costly method, especially when considering the ever-increasing number of checks requiring processing. Recognition's first TRACE system was delivered to the First National City Bank in New York City in 1973.

Also in 1973, Recognition developed the prototype of another significant new optical scanning device, the OCR WAND handheld reader. This compact scanner was designed to be attached to point-of-sale terminals in the retail environment where it would be "waved" across human-readable (OCR font-printed) merchandise tags on items to capture the desired data. Information such as size, color, stock number and price of the item would be entered into a central computer, allowing store department managers and buyers to maintain an accurate record of sales and inventory.

The OCR WAND Reader could interface with virtually every point-of-sale terminal manufactured. By 1980, over 70,000 of these readers had been installed in retail environments, worldwide. Among the large retailing companies currently using these handheld readers in the United States are Sears Roebuck, J. C. Penny, and Montgomery Ward.

The late 1970's were no less a period of Recognition's OCR product innovations than the 1960's and early 1970's. As the decade drew to a close, the company was offering current and prospective customers a wide range of optical scanning and closely related equipment for numerous applications.

Combining the TRACE system with the first use of image processing technology in automated check processing, Recognition introduced the TRACE Image ("TRIM") system in May, 1979. This innovation, which combined OCR with other state-of-the-art technologies, enabled banks to implement check truncation on customer checking accounts, producing economic benefits for the banks as well as better services to their customers. By the end of 1979, Recognition had obtained orders from two major United State banks for the installation of two of these new OCR/Image processing systems.

Observations from the 1977 OCRUA Summer Conference and this survey of REI's progress during the 1970's demonstrated that the decade was a very fruitful one for OCR's continuing progress as a "mature" data entry technology. As Arnold Keller editorialized so perceptively early in 1980, "OCR is alive and well". However, as the new decade began, the question still remained: "Where will OCR go from here"?

Chapter Eight

OCR In the Age of Instant Response

The theme of the January, 1980 conference of the Optical Character Recognition Users Association was "Increasing Data Entry Productivity Through OCR". In truth, no theme could have been more appropriate for that convocation of OCR equipment users and vendors since increasing productivity had already asserted itself as an overriding theme of all American business and industry as the many economic challenges of the 1980's were confronted.

Alarmingly declining rates of productivity improvement caused by the increased costs of manpower and materials, the high costs and limited supplies of energy resources, and the expensive compliance with government regulations had placed the United States far behind Japan and many nations of Western Europe in the endless competition to provide goods and services at the lowest possible costs. As clearly evidenced by the American automobile industry, for example, American consumers were turning in droves towards foreign-made cars to obtain the best value and economy of performance for their inflation-squeezed dollars. Simply stated, for a variety of reasons American goods and services were no longer being produced as efficiently as they once were and as they had to be to remain competitive.

A similar situation prevailed in the data processing industry. During the previous two decades, the cost to process one million bytes of information had declined sharply, from about $40 to only four cents. The cost for storing one million bytes of information for one month had dropped from $64 to $1.80. And, data processing hardware costs had dipped by more than 15 percent since 1977. However, also since 1977, data entry processing costs had also increased by approximately 14 percent yearly, and the cost to manually enter one million characters of information had risen over the past twenty years from $300 to more than $650.

Application of cost-intensive manpower to data entry was the primary reason for cost increases. The mechanical transfer of information via manual key entry was both expensive and time-consuming. Moreover, the cost for data processing personnel was forecasted to rise rapidly since data processing needs were expected to multiply drastically during the 1980's. Consequently, data entry remains one of the critical ''productivity targets'' in the information processing industry.

As early as 1961, data entry was disparagingly referred to as data processing's ''input bottleneck''. More recently, a published survey indicated that data entry represented a significant portion of data processing expenditures: approximately ten to 25 percent of total data processing budgets. And it is interesting to observe that, while American industrial productivity had increased by about 90 percent during the past ten years, the productivity of office workers had plodded along at a very disappointing four percent rate of improvement.

In 1980, 45 million Americans were classified as ''office workers''. By 1985 the total figure is projected to surpass 50 million. It is plainly apparent that increasingly efficient methods for data entry will have to be determined and will have to gain widespread acceptance if the ''input bottleneck'' is to be eliminated. Optical character recognition equipment manufacturers will need to address this problem directly during the decade ahead in order to help increase the productivity of data entry and to ensure their companies' profitability as well as, in many cases, their survival.

However, many of the "ancient" attitudes towards the conversion to cost-effective, productive OCR methods of data entry still persist. As Arnold Keller wrote soon after the 1980 Winter OCRUA Conference, "Many data processing professionals remain creatures of habit. They had cut their data processing teeth on 80-column cards, and the wisdom of change had seldom occurred. Even today, the card still retains an aura of respectability." There were six billion tab cards sold in 1979. It is apparent that this "tab card" mentality will have to be abandoned if OCR is to assume its rightful, earned role in increasing data entry productivity. Data processing management will have to be conscientious enough to give OCR the chance it deserves.

By early 1980, there were over thirty different companies supplying more than 80 different OCR products to users in the United States alone. Worldwide, more than 5,000 OCR systems were installed with an equivalent value of over $300 million. As stated previously, more than 70,000 OCR handheld readers were also in use. By 1982, this installed base of OCR equipment is estimated to grow to over 25,000 systems valued at more than $750 million and the total number of handheld scanners used is predicted to exceed 200,000.

The United States market for OCR products is forecast to expand at a compounded rate of 20 percent per year over the next five years (39 percent) in terms of units. OCR equipment manufacturers have the right to be "bullish" about their products and technology. The often-mentioned "Office of Tomorrow" cries out loudly for more and better OCR systems.

Business is entering a period that is being accurately referred to as the "Age of Instant Response". In the future, which in some instances is already here, many office workers and administrators alike will be equipped with only a single multiple-purpose terminal. Offices are evolving into "total business environments" in which staff responsibilities are growing far less segmented than they were formerly. The office personnel of the 1980's and beyond will have to be better trained, better equipped and better informed about more aspects of their companies' work if their productive value is to keep in step with the information needs of a continuously intensifying, data-oriented business world.

By 1990, it is predicted that most offices will be totally equipped with information terminals, displays and minicomputers connected to networks. Many office buildings will have their own small, rooftop satellite antennae making worldwide information access instantaneous, dependable and inexpensive.

Another forecast is that in the next decade, there will be more than 900,000 word processing terminals in North America alone. Fiberoptic digital cables, carrying up to trillions of bits per second on a single fiber, will link North America to Europe. Datacommunications is expected to become a $22 billion industry.

However, terminals and related equipment will not relegate OCR to obsolescence because two of OCR's greatest strengths cannot be supplanted. OCR has the ability to enter data quickly and accurately into a data base. Optical scanning has demonstrated this capability.

As REI President and Chief Executive Officer, Jay Rodney Reese said during his keynote address to the 1980 Winter OCRUA Conference, "OCR has already become almost synonymous with 'information acquisition'. As we enter the 1980's, this demonstrated capability of OCR must and will become even more apparent''.

In addition, Reese stressed the persistent need for smaller and more standardized OCR products, rather than totally customized ''one-of-a-kind'' systems. Achieving this goal, he explained, would benefit the OCR market not only by lowering the prices of optical scanning systems, but would also make OCR and its allied technologies available to many new and different kinds of businesses, inevitably leading to more widespread use of OCR-readable documents. . .and, subsequently, to the interchangeability of standardized documents among different types of businesses which would lead, in turn, to far less paperwork.

As OCR enters the 1980's, there are limitless opportunities for its application throughout our paper-oriented world. Numerous new horizons spread out before the OCR industry, both in those areas where this technology has been playing a significant role for many years and on previously unexplored horizons.

One of the currently leading exponents for much greater application of OCR is the United States Postal Service which, for more than three decades, has been actively interested or involved, to some extent, in the uses of OCR and its related technologies to read and sort letter mail more efficiently. It should also be noted that a similar interest exists in Europe and Canada for OCR mail sorting technology as well.

OCR systems are presently being used successfully to read and sort the mails in two European nations, France and Holland. However, OCR will soon be used far more extensively in America as the United States Postal Service implements their plan involving a nine-digit ZIP code.

Under this plan, the USPS will assign a nine-digit ZIP code to every business which regularly receives at least ten pieces of letter mail daily. Postage incentives will be offered to businesses to encourage them to fully utilize the new, longer ZIP codes, just as they are now being offered for using standardized sizes of envelopes for their mail.

Implementation plans for this new system call for the adoption of rules, assignment of additional ZIP code numbers, and the initial acquisition of basic equipment to make the program feasible. By 1984, the Postal Service expects the transition to the new, extended ZIP system to be virtually complete and fully operative.

According to Postmaster General William F. Bolger, the USPS plans to obtain optical character recognition and bar code recognition equipment worth more than $600 million. Once the nine-digit code comes into common use, postage rate increases predictably will be less dramatic or will occur less frequently. Since the Postage Service will be able to handle the same or even greater quantities of mail with less manpower and because manpower accounts for approximately 90 percent of the postal budget, the post office will be able to process the mail at a much lower cost. To phrase this another way, OCR will have a major impact on increasing the productivity of the Postal Service.

More efficient reading and sorting of letter mail is just one of the many ways OCR can contribute to our society during the years ahead. An ever-increasing presence of OCR will most certainly be felt in new, far-reaching applications in many additional areas of banking, retailing, government, health care, payment processing and office environments. Just as the use of computers has blossomed making more information available during the past 30 years, so will techniques evolve using OCR to better control the speed and accuracy of entering data into these computers.

In the early 1980's there was a strong market trend in data processing toward distributed processing, mini-computers and "home" computers. Similarly, in data entry there was an increasing response to the need for smaller configurations to meet smaller applications. Table-top, single page readers, wand and slot readers and smaller machines began to appear to meet these needs. By continuing this trend, OCR, creatively applied for specifiic applications, is destined to fulfill and surpass many of its expectations during the 1980's.

Historically, OCR has been an exciting, compelling technology that has inspired and challenged the imaginations of far-sighted individuals for many, many years. OCR is here to stay and is ready for new applications, new environments and new successes.

Jacob C. Rabinow is an OCR pioneer and inventor who worked for many years at the National Bureau of Standards (NBS) in Washington, DC where he was the Chief of the Mechanical Ordinance Division. In addition to his responsibility as Chief, he actively pursued unique creative activities in the fields of electronic computers, magnetic recorders, and OCR devices. In 1952, he built a working prototype of an OCR system at NBS. The output of this system was a portable typewriter which printed the characters as they were read. Compared to today's equipment this early prototype was primitive; it required more than a minute to read each alphanumeric character.

According to Jacob Rabinow, "the great pioneer in the OCR art was David Sheppard who founded the Intelligent Machine Research Corporation (IMR) to develop and build OCR equipments." Dr. Sheppard, who is now the Chairman of the Board of Directors of Cognitronics Corp., and who enthusiastically attacked data entry problems, is credited with developing the first practical OCR Scanner in 1951. It was Sheppard's IMR Corporation which manufactured and installed the first commercial optical character reader for Reader's Digest in 1954. The application at Reader's Digest was to convert typewritten documents into punched cards for the magazine's subscription department. IMR also developed the first OCR page reader for the USAF in Rome, New York in 1959. This machine had the capability of reading a full upper and lower case alpha-numeric font.

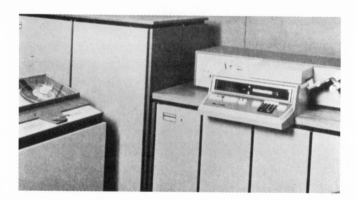

In 1959, Farrington Manufacturing Company purchased IMR. This acquisition catapulted Farrington to the forefront of the then embryonic optical scanning industry. The Farrington Research Department, in effect, was IMR. In early 1960, Farrington delivered the first document carrier to Arizona Public Service Company in Phoenix, Arizona. Those vacuum tube machines were the forerunners of the Farrington 3010 document carrier and 3030 page reader.

OP SCAN Model 70, an optical mark reader introduced in 1960.

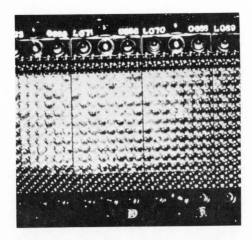

From 1961 to 1964 REI researched and developed this **Real World OCR Reader** which was announced in 1962 as the "Electronic Retina Computing reader (ERCR)". The Electronic Retina, the eye, of the ERCR was invented and developed by Israel Sheinberg, another OCR pioneer, and one of REI's first engineers. He patterned the design of the Electronic Retina after the human eye, knowledge he gained as a medical student before turning his talent to engineering. This invention, based on the same light-sensing principle as the human eye, reads the complete character image and distinguishes shades of gray.

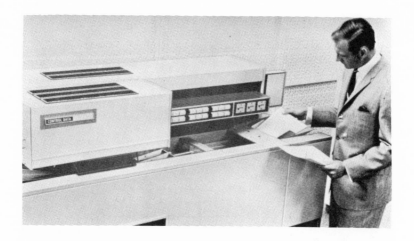

In January 1964, Rabinow Engineering Company became the Rabinow Division of the Control Data Corporation (CDC). An early commercial machine at CDC was the 915. The first 915 was installed at the Crocker Citizens National Bank in San Francisco in October, 1965. CDC announced the 935 document carrier in October, 1968 which also used a columnar scanner.

In 1965, IBM delivered a high-speed multifont reader, the IBM 1975, to the Social Security Administration. In 1968, the IBM 1287, a document reader was introduced followed by the 1288 page reader later the same year.

In 1967, REI announced the Ink-Jet Printer, with no moving parts, to print coded information on the back of documents previously read by OCR on the ERCR. In 1967, REI also announced the high-speed Bar Code Reader Sorter System to be used in conjunction with the IJP. (BCR/S-I sorted at 1800 DPM). The first IJP and BCRS were installed in the British General Post Office in late 1967. The first U.S. installation was in the spring of 1968 at Texaco in Houston. In 1968, the high-speed BCRS was announced by REI. At 2400 DPM it was the fastest document sorter in the world.

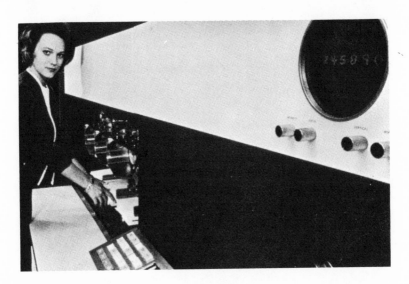

In 1968, IBM introduced the 1287 (Document Reader).

In 1968, IBM introduced the 1288, OCR Page Reader.

In 1970, REI announced the Input 80 Model A. It was a state of the art Page Reader with an Integrated Retina.

In 1971, REI introduced the OCR/S 2000; a high-speed OCR Transaction Processing System primarily for the Scandinavian Giro's. This system was capable of processing Giro documents at rates up to 2400 documents per minute. The initial OCR/S 2000 was shipped to the Swedish Postal Bank during the first quarter of 1972.

In 1972, the Input 80 Models B and C were introduced with the Total Data Entry capability. These readers used new technology integrated retinas and high reliability lower priced peripherals.

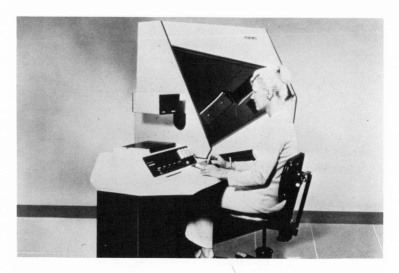

OBM - Laser I, vacuum feed, laser scanner, matrix-feature RU introduced in 1975.

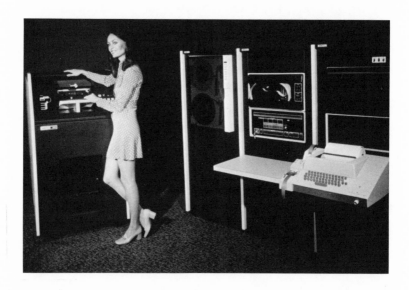

Scan-Data 2250, friction feed, flying spot scanner, feature Mixed Media On-line to Scanplex. (1975)

Appendix A

OCR List of Terms

Accordion fold A term used in binding for two or more parallel folds of paper which open like an accordion. (Usually from a line printer)

Accumulator The register and associated equipment in the arithmetic unit of the computer in which arithmetical and logical operations are performed.

2. A unit in a digital computer where numbers are totalled. The device stores an operand and upon receipt of a second operand performs the indicated operation and stores the result where the first operand has been; i.e. result accumulates.

Accuracy The degree of freedom from error; i.e., the degree of conformity to truth or to a rule. How well does the system read?

Adjacent characters Two OCR characters are adjacent if printed on the same line and their character spacing reference lines are separated by less than one character space.

Alignment edge The guide edge of a scanning form which is used for alignment so that the printed character line will be parallel to the direction of scanning.

Alpha character Those letters (A to Z) in a specific font. Numeric characters (0 to 9) or special characters (period, comma, asterisk and others) are not included.

Alpha/numeric characters The characters that include letters of the alphabet (A to Z) and Numerals (0 to 9). Special characters are not included.

Angstrom Unit of measurement, 1/10 of a nanometer, used for light wave lengths to scale the color spectrum. Commonly refer to when determining spectral response of optical readers.

ANSI American National Standards Institute. This association has been and is developing standards for data processing and optical character recognition for the United States.

ANSI subcommittee X3A1 The subcommittee is responsible for the drafting and formalization of American National OCR Standards. CBEMA is secretariat for X3. X3A1 is a subcommittee for X3.

> Example: X3.17 OCR-A Font
> X3.49 OCR-B Font
> X3.45 Character Set for Handprinting
> X3.99 OCR Print Quality

Application The problem to which a scanning system is applied.

Array An arrangement of elements in one or more dimensions such as the photo diode array in the recognition unit of a scanner.

Ascender That part of the character which rises above the main body, as in 'D'.

Aspect ratio The ratio of the forms vertical dimension to its horizontal dimension. This term is also applied to characters where it is the ratio of the character height to the character width.

Back printing Printing on the reverse side of a scanning form.

Background color (ink) See 'Drop-Out-Color (ink)', 'Non-Read Color (ink)', 'Reflective Color (ink)', & 'Blind Color (ink)'.

Background reflectance A brightness measurement of paper, expressed as a percent of a reflectance standard.

Backspace To move one unit in the reverse or backward direction as opposed to moving one unit in the forward position direction. This generally refers to machine printing by either a typewriter or line printer.

Bar code Machine readable binary coding system consisting of vertical marks or bars and spaces.

Bar code printer An impact printer in which the type slugs print a complete bar code representing an individual character. A series of bar codes can be printed to represent a complete numerical sequence.

Bar code reader An optical scanning system that can read documents containing bar codes.

Bar code reader sorter an optical scanning system that can read and sort documents containing bar codes.

Barium sulphate $= BaSO_4$ A standard of reflectance used to calibrate instruments for the measurements of reflectance of paper or ink. Also, see MGO, or magnesium oxide.

Bar printer An impact printer in which the type slugs are carried on a type bar.

Bark mark See 'Dirt'

Base line The reference line used to specify the nominal relative vertical position of characters or marks printed on the same line.

Basis weight (paper) The weight in pounds of a ream (500 sheets) of paper cut to a given standard size for that grade.

Batch A group of records or documents considered as a single unit for the purpose of processing.

2. A number of records or documents grouped together for the purpose of processing as a single unit.

Batch processing A technique by which items to be processed are collected into groups prior to processing and controlled by batch identity.

Batch total The sum of certain quantities, used to verify accuracy of operations on a particular batch of records; e.g., in a payroll calculation, the batches might be departments and batch totals would be number of employees in the department, total hours worked in the department, total pay for the department.

Binary A numbering system based on 2's, rather than 10's, using only the digits 0 and 1.

2. A characteristic, property or condition in which there are but two possible states e.g., the binary numbering system using 2 as its base and using only the digits zero (0) and one (1). (Related to binary coded decimal, and clarified by number systems.)

Binary coded decimal (BCD) Pertaining to a decimal notation in which the individual decimal digits are each represented by a binary code group, i.e., in the 8-4-2-1 coded decimal notation the digits of the number twenty-three are represented as 0010 0011. (In pure binary notation, the value of twenty-three is represented by 10111.)

Bit An abbreviation of binary digit.

2. A single character in a binary number.

3. A single pulse in a group of pulses.

4. A unit of information capacity of a storage device. The capacity in bits is the logarithm to the base two of the number of possible states of the device.

Blank space A character used to indicate space in which nothing is printed.

Blink color (ink) See 'Non-Read Color (ink)', 'Reflective Color (ink)' & 'Non-Scan color (ink)'.

Block A group of data considered as a unit by virtue of their being stored in successive storage locations.

2. The set of locations or tape positions in which a block of data, as defined above, is stored or recorded.

Body (ink) A term referring to the viscosity, consistency or covering power of an ink or vehicle.

Brightness In paper, a characteristic of white paper measured in terms of reflectance in the blue and violet portions of the spectrum.

Bulk (paper) The degree of thickness of paper.

Burst To separate continuous-form paper into discrete sheets.

Burster Forms handling device for mechanically separating continuous forms at the cross perforation, usually using two sets of pressure rollers rotating at different speeds.

Business form Any material which has been printed or otherwise especially prepared in a predetermined format for the primary purpose of facilitating the entry of variable information. Such written information may be hand or machine entered. Blank paper may be included, especially if it is continuous and has undergone some manufacturing operation such as punching or perforating, etc.

2. More specifically, document bearing instructions with repetitive information printed in fixed positions to save writing and reference time.

Byte A group of binary digits usually processed as a unit, i.e. an 8 bit byte or 6 bit byte.

Caliper (paper) The thickness of a sheet of paper—usually expressed in thousandths of an inch.

Cancel character An accuracy control character on some typing elements used to in dictate that the data with which it is associated are in error or are to be disregarded.

Carbon Paper coated on one or both sides used in a formset to effect image transfer under pressure.

Carbon black The color pigment used in most black carbons and black inks.

Carbon paper A tissue coated with a pigment for the purpose of transferring an image under impact or pressure.

Carbonized paper Paper part of a form to which a carbon coating has been directly applied to the back side. It is used in specialized instances to effect good write-through at low cost.

Carbonless paper Any paper stock coated, manufactured or treated to provide part to part imaging without use of carbon interleaves or carbon type coating. Mated-chemical carbonless systems require contact of two paper surfaces each with a different chemical coating which reacts chemically under impact of pressure to form a visible image on one surface ('coated front' or CF surface). Self-contained chemical carbonless paper ('self imaging') has the two materials coated on or manufactured into the same sheet. Mechanical transfer carbonless paper relies on physical transfer of pigmented materials. Mated-mechanical carbonless systems require contact of two paper surfaces like the mated-chemical except there is a physical transfer requirement. Mechanical self-contained has a pigmented under surface which is revealed when a lighter colored surface coating is rendered transparent by pressure or impact.

Card set Cards and forms, bound in a manner that provides multiple copies of source data.

Carriage return (CR) The operation that prepares for the next character to be printed or displayed at the specified first position on the same line.

Cathode ray tube display (CRT display) A device that presents data in visual form by means of controlled electron beams.
2. The data display produced by the device as in (1).

CBEMA Computer and Business Equipment Manufacturer's Association, sponsor of the × 3 committee and × 3 subcommittees.

Centerline stroke (character) The line drawn between the two average edges of a character and which follows the character shape.

Central processing unit (CPU) A unit of a computer that includes circuits controlling the interpretation and execution of instructions. Synonymous with central processor, main frame.

Chain printer An impact printer in which the type slugs are carried by links of a revolving chain.

Character An elementary printed mark that is used to represent data. A character is often in the form of a graphic spatial arrangement of connected or adjacent strokes. For example A through Z are the alpha characters of the English language.

Character alignment The placement of a printed or typed character in relation to its intended position.

Character boundry The largest rectangle with sides parallel and perpendicular to the document reference edge which can be drawn tangential to the character outline.

Character density The number of characters in a line of print per unit of length.

Character erase A graphic shape that will delete a single character or space.

Character misread The incorrect identification of a valid readable character (a substitution).

Character outline The graphic patterns established by the edges of a printed image.

Character reader A machine which senses graphic shapes on paper, film or other media, and converts them into machine language signals.

Character recognition Identifying, reading, or encoding a printed character by various means which include magnetic, optical mechanical and others.
2. The technology of sensing and translating into a machine language, characters which are written or printed to be read by human beings.

Character set An agreed set of representations, called characters, from which selections are made to denote and distinguish data. The total number of characters in a given set if fixed; e.g., a set may include the numerials 0 to 9, letters A to Z, punctuation marks and a blank or space, combination thereof, or all.

Character spacing The center to center distance between adjacent characters, marks or bars. The two basic values often specified are the minimum and maximum distances permissable for proper recognition.

Character dimensions Characteristics of printed data, including the height and width of a character as well as the stroke width of a character.

Character skew A character, whose vertical centerline is not perpendicular to the reference edge of the document, is skewed. The angle formed by the centerline and a line perpendicular to the document reference edge must have certain tolerance levels dependent upon the machine.

Character stroke width The distance between average edges of a character element.

Character style (font) A distinctive construction, with no restriction as to size, that is common to a group of characters. Different sizes of a given characterstyle are proportional in all respects.

Check digit One or more redundant digits in the number as a self checking or error detecting code to minimize misreads.
2. An extra or redundant digit related to the group of digits to be checked by a specific rule for double check.

Cleanliness A measure of the absence of process dirt in paper.

Clear area A specified area that is to be kept free of printing or any other markings not related to machine reading.

Clock mark See 'timing mark'.

Clock track A series of clock marks in a track on which a pattern of signals is recorded to provide a timing reference.

Collate To assemble the various parts of a form set.

Collator In production, the machine used for assembling the part of a business form either from sheets or from paper and carbon rolls.

Color The spectral appearance of the image, dependent upon the spectral composition of incident light.

Column The vertical arrangement of data or other expressions. Contrast with row.

Compile The conversion of a relatively machine independent source program into specific machine language routines. 2. To develop or produce a logically or sequentially ordered machine language program from a series of mnemonics or symbolic operation codes or statements. Special compilers are utilized to perform this transformation from non-machine language to machine language.

Composition Assembly of camera-ready art (type rules and other form components such as screens, logos, etc.) to be used in the production of the form.

Consecutive numbering Numbers preprinted in series on forms, normally by mechnical numbering machines which are mounted on the press or collator.

Constraint boxes See 'guide boxes.'

Continuous form Forms attached to one another vertically to permit continuous, uniform feeding to a printing device.

Contrast The difference in reflectance between an image and the background upon which it is placed.

Controller A device driving hardware or software system segments.

Control character A character whose occurrence in a particular context initiates, modifies or stops an operation; e.g., a character that indicates the start of a field.

Control panel A part of control console that contains manual controls.

Control total A sum of numbers accumulated from specified record fields of a batch of records, determined repetitiously during the processing operations so that any discrepancy from the control indicates an error.

Convert To change the representation of data from one form to another without changing the information they convey.

Coordinates The divisions of the scanning area.

Copy Any furnished material 'typewritten manuscript, layout, artwork, etc.) to be used in the production of the business form.

2. To reproduce by some means.

Corner cut Diagonal cut on one corner of a form so proper alignment can be maintained in a batch of documents.

Counter A mechanical or electronic device cleared manually or by program control and incremented by program control to record information useful to the operation, such as number of lines scanned.

Crash imprinting Imprinting of numbers and other data through all copies of a multiple part formset by mechanical numbering machines and relief plates on a collator.

Crossfooting The accumulation of the columns of figures or fields from a matrix wherein each horizontal line has a total and the sum accumulated equals the sum of totals.

Curve tracing or following This scanning technique is accomplished by tracing the character's curvature; the recognition unit determines certain features which it used to identify the character.

Custom form Form manufactured to client order in all respects as compared to stock form, imprint.

Cut sheet Individual form-sheets not printed in continuous form fashion or the end product of a continuous forms press employing a sheetcut-off.

Data A general term used to denote any or all facts, numbers or letters any symbols that refer to or describe an object, idea, condition, situation or other factors. It connotes basic elements of information which can be processed or produced by acomputer.

Data collection The act of bringing data from one or more points to a central point.

Data field A set of graphics which can be identified as a unit of data.

Debug To locate and correct any problem in a computer program or equipment.

Decollator Forms handling device for separating the parts of a continuous form; normally carbon paper, if present, will be removed at the same time.

Deleaver Forms handling device for removing one-time carbon from continuous forms.

Delete character A control character used primarily to obliterate an erroneous or unwanted character.

Delimiter See 'field mark'.

Descender That part of the letter which extends below the main body, as in 'p'.

De-skewing fingers A set of mechanical retractable fingers extending perpendicularly up into the path of the document in an optical transport system, which are retracted to allow passage of the document if the document is not skewed.

Diffuse reflectance See 'reflectance'.

Digit One of the N symbols of integral value, ranging from 0 to N-1 inclusive, in a system of numbering with radix N; for example, the ten digits 0, 1, 2, 3, 4, 5, 6, 7, 8, 9 in the decimal system.

Dirt Nonreflective foreign particles in a sheet of paper which adversely affect the sheet's reflectance and optical readability.

Document A sheet of paper containing a representation of stored information. Often provides a complete unit record of information.

Document reader A scanning device that scans one to five lines of data in fixed locations on a document at a single pass. Generally, re-scanning or a portion of the document is not possible, one direction of the scan being provided by movement of the form past the reading head. The forms used generally don't exceed 8 ¾ inches in width by 4 ¼ inches in depth. Also see page reader.

Document reference edge A specified edge with respect to which the alignment of data is defined. (See reference edge).

Document registration time the time lapse between the trailing edge of one document until the next document is ready for reading at the read station.

Dot matrix printer Print-out device which forms characters by printing dots commonly within 5 × 5 or 7 × 7 grid pattern. The most common small dot matrix printers are character printers which have a 7 or 9-wireprint head ('wire printer'). Other, non-wire techniques are used in various matrix line and character printers.

Double detector A photoelectric device used by some optical equipment which prevents two or more documents from being transported at the same time.

Double document detection A method to prevent transport of more than one document at a time using a sample slot or some other device.

Double face carbon Carbon paper coated on both sides.

Drier In inkmaking, any substance added to hasten drying.

Drop-out colors (ink) Reflective colors of ink used for lines and instructions on scanner designed forms. The purpose of such colors is to produce images which are invisible to optical scanners, but visible to people utilizing the forms. (See non-read color (ink), blind color (ink) & reflective color (ink).

Drum printer A line printer in which the type are mounted on a rotating drum that contains a full character set for each printing position.

Dry offset Printing process which uses a blanket (like conventional offset) for transferring the image from the plate to the paper; unlike conventional offset, the plate has a relief image and requires no dampening.

ECMA Acronymn for European Computer Manufacturer's Association which sponsors European Manufacturer's standards development activities for OCR.

Edge See 'document reference edge'.

Edit To rearrange information for machine input or output, i.e., to rearrange, delete, select or insert any needed data, symbols or characters.

2. To rearrange data or information. Editing may involve the deletion of unwanted data; the selection of pertinent data, the application of format techniques, the insertion of symbols such as page numbers and typewriter characters, the application of standard processes such as zero suppression and the testing of data for accuracy through use of a number of techniques such as range checks or check digits.

EDP Electronic data processing.

Electric typewriter A hand operated, electric powered individual printing device having the property that almost every operation of the machine after the keys have been depressed is performed by electric rather than manual power.

Elite A class of typewriter fonts normally providing 12 characters to the linear inch.

Embossing The condition of the paper when the type slugs have dented or cut the document with the outline of the characters. Embossing can be seen or felt on the reverse side of typed edges.

Encode To convert data by the use of a code or a coded character set in such a manner that reconversion to the original form is possible.

Encoder A device that encodes data.

Erase character Same as 'delete character'. Error in optical recognition, an error is generally defined as the in correct recognition of an image. (A misread).

Error rate The ratio of the number of documents in which one or more errors occur to the total number of documents read.

Extraneous ink Any spot appearing within the 'read' area, but outside the image itself, caused by streaking, smear or splatter. Extraneous ink spots can be caused either in the process of forms manufacturing or while entering data. This can result in less optimum readability.

Face The printing surface of a piece of type.

Fanfold Paper or card forms attached trailing edge to leading edge for continuous feeding.

Fastening Device or technique for holding the elements of a continuous formset together; normally performed on the collator or as a final bindery operation. Fastening is described in terms of type (staple, glue, sew, crimp), by positioning (marginal, corner, perforation, sectional), or by function (permanent, flexible, temporary).

Feed belt A belt used to feed documents into a transport system to be read and sorted.

Feed wheels A pair of wheels, rotating in opposite directions, between which documents are transported by friction.

Felt side Top side or smooth side of a sheet of paper—normally the side on which printing is placed.

Field Refers to a group of characters treated as a unit of information.

Field mark A mark or symbol printed in red ink used to identify field boundaries.

Field-prepared form A data entry form prepared at multiple points, for optical reading at one or more central locations.

Field-separator mark see 'field mark'.

File hold punching A hold made near some edge of a form to permit it to be placed in a collator or final bindery punched.

Flow The ability of an ink to spread over a surface or into a thin film.

Flow chart Graphic representation of a system, data flow, etc. using labeled symbols connected by lines.

Fluoresence Optical brighteners added to paper to enhance its whiteness or brightness to the human eye in normal lighting. Because they absorb and emit light energy at different wavelengths, they can cause erratic reflectance values.

Flying spot scanner In OCR, a device employing a moving spot of light to scan a sample space; the transmitted or reflected light is sensed by a photoelectric transducer.

Font A complete assortment of type of one size and style; e.g., ANSI OCR-A size I, ANSI OCR-B size I, E13B, Pica, Elite, 7B, etc. In OCR, a distinctive construction with no restriction as to size, that is common to a group of characters. Different sizes of the given character style are proportional in all respects.

Form Documents, pages, or journal tapes used for optical data entry.

Format A predetermined arrangement of images, fields, lines, punctuation, page numbers, etc.
2. A defined arrangement of words, totals, characters, and headings for a desired clear presentation of data or print out.

Format identifier or number A character or series of characters that are usually preprinted, but may be hand printed or machine printed, that are optically read to signify a reading pattern or form identification which is under program control. These are normally repetitive data. For this purpose a symbol (e.g., &, --, *, etc.) is classified as a character.

Forms analysis The art or science of resolving what goes on a form. More specifically, forms analysis can be defined as 'A means of determining if a form is necessary and if so, what type of form it should be, what physical characteristics it should have and what data it should contain.

Forms control Part of business management relating to analysis, standardization and regulation for forms design and use; may include forms purchasing and inventorying as a centralized function.

Forms design The art or science of resolving how to best arrange and present the information on a form.

Forms handling equipment Equipment used to process (or assist in processing) forms after they have been written.

2. More specifically, machines to process continuous forms after execution such as bursters and decollators.

Framing A printing phenomenon associated most commonly with chain and train printer in which a carbon 'frame' surrounds a printed character.

Free form A data-entry form in which data appear in variable length fields without the use of preprinted symbols or guides.

Full matrix scan A scanning method wherein light reflected from a graphic shape is projected upon a rectangular grid of photoelectric elements.

Fuzz Fibers projecting from the surface of a sheet of paper.

Gloss A phenomenon related to the specular reflection of incident light as opposed to diffuse or scattered reflection. The effect of gloss is to reflect more of the incident light in a specular manner and to scatter less. Paper gloss is considered undesirable for optical systems since it will change the effective brightness of the paper, thus affecting the print contrast signal.

Grain direction the direction of the fibers in paper composition. 'Long grain' means that the long dimension of the document is parallel to the direction of paper stock movement through a paper-making mill. 'Short grain' denotes that the short dimension of the document is parallel to the direction of paper travel through the mill.

Graphic A symbol produced by a process such as handwriting, drawing, or printing.

Grid Two mutually orthogonal sets of parallel lines used for measuring or specifying character or mark images.

Groundwood paper Economy grade of paper sometimes used for forms, most often continuous stock forms; groundwood forms papers normally contain a mixture of mechanical wood pulp (groundwood) and chemical pulp. Not to be used for OCR applications.

Group erase An OCR graphic shape used to delete a group or string of three or more characters.

Guard band Can be the same as margin, clear band or border.

Guide boxes Preprinted reflective ink patterns used to control placement of handprinted characters or marks on scanner forms.

Guide edge See 'reference edge'.

Handprint In OCR, a set of characters, printed by hand, which conform to certain shape and size specifications, and which can be recognized by an optical character reader.

Handprint boxes Guides used to control entry of handprinted characters.

Header A file record that contains common, constant or identifying in formation for a group of records which are to follow.

Head margin The white space above the first line on the page.

High speed mirror The device used for vertical scanning which receives reflections from the low speed mirror and transmits the reflections to a photoelectric transducer.

Mopper A device that holds cards or documents and makes them available to a feed mechanism. (Contrasts with stacker).

Horizontal spacing Horizontal spacing is defined as the space between the vertical centerlines of adjacent scannable images.

Hot spot carbonizing Application of carbon ink to portions of the back of a form, as a technique for obtaining selective write-through with interleaves.

Illegal character A character that is not contained within the equipment's vocabulary. (Character set and font).

Image The outline configuration of a graphic shape.

Image dissector A mechanical or electronic transducer that sequentially detects the level of light in different areas of a completely illuminated sample space.

Impact printer A printer in which printing is the result of mechanical impacts.

Imprinter A device that uses embossed cards to imprint data on a document via a carbon transfer.

Imprinting The act of using an imprinter.
2. The output of any imprinter.

Infrared response (IR) A type of optical system used in some optical devices, which operates in the red-infrared region of the frequency spectrum.

Ink bleed The capillary flow of ink beyond the original edges of a printed image which can cause rejects and misreads.

Ink smudge The displacement of ink under shear beyond the original edges of a printed image which can cause rejects and misreads.

Ink jet printer Type of non-impact printer making use of an array of tiny nozzles and associated deflection plates which emit streams of ink drop lets and directs them onto plain paper to form characters or graphics.

Input device—optical reader This device optically reads printed and typewritten material and directly converts it into a compatible format for direct entry into the computer.

IOS International Organization for Standardization. This group promotes voluntary standards development for OCR on an international basis as ANSI does to the United States.

Journal tape Normally, the output format of cash registers and calculators; usually a continuous piece of paper.

Keyboard The area of a machine on which the printing and functional keys are arrayed.

Keyboard arrangement The position of the keys relative to one another and the arrangement of characters, and functions on them.

Keyboard layout The physical relationship of keys containing a character set on a keyboard.

Keypunch A device to record information on cards or tape by punching holes in the cards or tape to represent letters, digits, and special characters. 2. To operate a device for punching holes in cards or tape.

Label An attachment to an input document that changes the thickness of caliper of the paper stock.

Laser A condensed directed lightbeam of single frequency. This optical transmission technique could raise the speed of operation to rates measured in gigacycles (billions of cycles) per second.

Laser scanner An optical scanning device that uses the intense monochromatic light beam given off by a laser as its source of illumination.

Layout sheet Form with printed horizontal and vertical grids compatible with the method of writing used by the forms designer as a guide in drawing the form.

Leading edge Usually, the edge of a form first entering the read area.

Left justified Data is left justified when the left hand digit or character (or its sign) occupies the left hand position of the space allotted for that data.

Length The distance between the two edges of a form, measured perpendicular to a data line as the form is fed through an optical reader.

Lens See 'reading lens'.

Letterpress Printing process which employs a relief or raised, inked image which comes into direct contact with the material being printed. Letterpress printing can be performed from metal type or plates, rubber plates, or plastic plates; using rotary, flatbed or platen press.

Letter spacing The spacing between each letter of a word.

Light pipes Optical devices that carry light. Light pipes are sometimes used to carry reflected character images to photomultipliers.

Line boundary The smallest rectangle, with sides parallel and perpendicular to the reference edge, which contains all images of a line of print.

Line holes Series of holes running parallel with the edge of the web used to control the paper in a manufacturing machine (press or collator) form writing machine or forms handling equipment. Nominal specifications for line holes of

5/32 inch diameter, ½ inch center to center, and ¼ inch center to edge of paper. Also marginal punching, sprocket holes, feed holes.

Line printer An imaging device that prints all images of a line as a unit.

Line separation The vertical distance between the upper line boundary of a line of print and the lower line boundary for the line immediately above.

Line skew A line of printed data, oblique to the reference edge of the document, is skewed. A skewed line is acceptable to the reader only if the line remains within the tolerance of the machine design.

Line spacing The vertical distance between the average baseline of one line and the average baseline of the next line.

Lithography Printing process in which the printing and non-printing area on the printing plate are in the same plane (even surface). Works on the principle that oil and water do not mix.

Lockup space Image-free or non-printed areas across a form. Lockup space is necessary to lock the printing plate to the plate cylinder. Lockup space normally needed is ½ or ⅜ inch.

Logic The electronic components of optical recognition device wherein scan signal (analogues) are converted into corresponding machine language signals.

Long-vertical mark = **LVM** An OCR graphic shape used usually as a field delimiter (See field mark).

Lower case The small alpha character type font, as distinguished from the large alpha character or 'upper case'.

LPM Lines per minute, describing the speed for a forms writing machine.

Machine language A language designed for use by a machine without translation.

Machine readable Graphic shapes or symbols of a set which can be read or sensed by an optical device.

Magnesium oxide = **MGO** A standard of reflectance used to calibrate instruments for measuring the whiteness or reflectance of paper; now superseded by barium sulphate ($BaSO_4$). (Also, see barium sulphate).

Magnetic ink Ink containing particles of magnetic substance which can be detected or read by magnetic ink character recognition (MICR).

Main frame Synonym for central processing unit (CPU).

Manifold Adjective which in general forms industry usage denotes 'multiparts.'

Margin That border on the document in which printing will not be read by the scanner.

Mark read Method of optically reading pencil marks logically formatted on a form to be scanned for further processing. Also known as OMR.

Marking position The area designated to mark information on a mark read form. Also called a response position.

Matrix matching This technique stores the scanner signals in a digital register that is connected to a series of resistor matrices. Each matrix represents a single reference character. The other end of each matrix is connected to a second digital register, whose voltage outputs are representative of what should be obtained if the reference character were present. Recognition is based upon the resultant output voltage obtained from each matrix.

Mechanical disk scanner This type of scanner consists of a lens system, a rotating disk, a fixed aperture plate, and a photomultiplier. The characters to be read are flooded with light, which is reflected from the surface of the document onto a rotating disk via the lens system. The disk has apertures extending from its center toward it periphery. As the disk rotates, the aperture picks up light samples. A fixed aperture plate regulated the amount of light and directs the light into a photomultiplier. The photomultiplier tube converts the light samples into a signal pulse. By varying the voltage threshold, the photocell outputs can be adjusted for difference background colors. The scanner senses a character of data at a time.

Mechanical self-contained paper A carbonless paper that forms an image on impact by exposing a dark undercoating.

Mechanical servoing The process whereby a stepping motor moves the document being read forward or backward if the line of text is not centered within the optical reading areas, as determined by the recognition system.

MICR (Magnetic Ink Character Recognition) A common language used primarily within the banking industry consisting of 14 (E-13B) characters imprinted to high specifications using ink with iron oxide pigments, capable of being magnetized. E-13B characters can also be OCR readable by some OCR readers.

MIL Unit of measurement usually referring to thickness; 1/1000 inch (.001 inch).

Multi-font machine An optical scanning device which can read forms containing intermixed characters printed in a number of fonts. This approach eliminates the need to prebatch the input data by font prior to submission to the scanner.

Multiple font machine An optical scanning device which can read more than one type font, although only one type font may be read at any given time.

Multi-web press Press capable of printing, processing and collating two or more paper webs and necessary carbons in one pass to produce a finished form.

Nanometer Unit of measure used for specifying optical character reader wave lengths; one billionth of a meter or the same as millimicron. Referred to when specifying spectral response characteristics of optical readers.

Negative Film containing an image in which the values of the original artwork are reversed so the dark areas appear light & vice versa.

Noise Electronic variations in the scanner read head caused by miscellaneous nonreflective spots other than data to be read, such as dirt, black ink spots, holes, etc.

Non-freeze carbon One-time carbon paper designed for use in forms which are subjected to temperatures of near freezing or below.

Non-impact printer Printout device which does not rely upon mechanical impact to produce an image, using instead any variety of electronic techniques. Non-impact printers are described according to the type of media used (plain paper or coated paper) and by the process or physical phenomenon used (electrostate, thermal, ink jet, etc.).

Non-read color (ink) Any printing with a sufficiently high reflectance measurement to prohibit detection by the scanner. Non-read colors are used as visual guides that do not interfere with data reading. See 'dropout color (ink)', 'reflective color (ink)' or 'non scan color (ink)' & 'blind color (ink)'.

Non reflective color (ink) See 'read color (ink)', 'scan color (ink)'.

Non scan color (ink) See 'non read color (ink)', 'reflective color (ink)' & 'blind color (ink)'.

Numeric A graphic shape representing one of the 10 numerical character 0 through 9.

OBR See 'optical bar code recognition'.

OCR See 'optical character recognition'.

OCR-A OCR character set developed by ANSI and adopted as an American national standard in 1966. This standard is documented in ANSI X3.17-1977, American national standard character set and print quality for optical character recognition. The standard specifies three sizes, size I, size III and size IV.

OCR-B OCR character set originally developed by the European Computer Manufacturers Association (ECMA) and adopted by that organization's general assembly in 1965. OCR-B was also adopted by the International Organization of Standardization (ISO) in 1969. This character set as an American standard is contained in ANSI X3.49-1975, American national character set for optical character recognition (OCR-B). This standard specifies three sizes, size I, size III, and size IV.

Off-line Descriptive of a system and of the peripheral equipment or devices in a system which operate independently of mainframe.

Offset printing A process where the image is transferred from the plate cylinder to a blanket cylinder to the paper web. Offset lithography and dry offset of examples of offset printing.

OMR See 'optical mark recognition'.

One-time carbon Carbon paper designed to be used within a form for just one writing, then discarded. One time carbon is now virtually standard for most business forms applications. (Exception: most register forms and sales books).

On-line Descriptive of a system and peripheral equipment or devices in a system which are dependent upon a mainframe for control.

Opacity The property of paper that minimizes the show-through of printing from the back side or the next sheet.

Opaque ink An ink that covers nearly all color beneath it.

Optic Of or relating to vision or the eye, or any of the lenses, prisms or mirrors of an optical instrument.

Optical Acting by means of light or in accord with the principles of optics.

Optical brightener A material often added to paper during its manufacture to improve its brightness or whiteness. These materials can cause erratic reflectance values when used with optical scanners that are sensitive to the short wavelength portion of the spectrum. See fluorescence.

Optical bar code recognition (OBR) The recognition of valid machine produced binary coding system consisting of bars and spaces that when read by optical equipment is converted to machine language.

Optical character recognition (OCR) The recognition of valid machine and/or handprinted characters using the optical properties of the equipment and media. A reliable means of high speed automatic data entry where printed data is directly converted into a machine compatible language.

Optical mark recognition (OMR) The process of identification of marks by an optical scanner.

Optical path The path followed by light through an optical system.

Optical reader An information processing device that accepts prepared forms and converts data from them to computer output media.

Optical scanner Equipment system of hardware and/or software that scans optically and generates data for computer input. See OBR, OCR & OMR.

Optical type font Fonts which can be read by both people and machines.

Original The part of a formset usually in contact with a printing device.

Output stackers A mechanism that stacks documents or pages after they have passed through a machine. (See stackers).

Over printing Double printing; printing over an area that already has been printed.

Page reader An optical scanning device designed primarily to read pages with many lines of data printed on a page.

Pantone matching system (PMS) Color matching system for printing inks using color identification numbers for specification and communication. In some cases OCR ink colors are specified by a PMS number.

Paper caliper The thickness of a given sheet of paper. See caliper.

Paper grain See 'grain direction'.

Paper reflectance See 'reflectance'.

Paper smoothness See 'smoothness'.

Paper weight The weight of paper in pounds for a given number of sheets in a specified size.

> Example: 20 lbs. paper (commercial)
> 500 17 × 22 inch sheets weight 20 pounds

Pattern recognition The identification of shapes, forms or configurations by comparing the shape scanned to an electronic pattern.

PCR See 'print contrast ratio'.

PCS See 'print contrast signal'.

Perforation Series of cuts or holes entered into a form to weaken it for tearing or bursting.

Photoelectric cell A cell whose electrical properties are modified by the action of light.

Photomultiplier An electronic device which converts light into electrical signals. Its current increases as the amount of light energy (whiteness) received increases.

Pica A class of type written fonts, usually spaced 10 to the inch.

Pinfeed Method of driving and controlling a form by engaging pins with line holes; in forms writing or handling equipment, pinfeeding is accomplished by a tractor mechanism (pins mounted on a chain or belt), sprocket (toothed wheel), or pinfeed platen.

Pitch Horizontal character spacing.

Platen Part of a printout device or typewriter which supports the paper against the impact of the type or print wires.

Porosity The property of paper which permits or resists the passage of air through a paper sheet. A very important factor in the vacuum feeding mechanism in certain readers.

POS An abbreviation for point of sales data entry systems where actual transactions are recorded by terminals operating on-line to a central computer. These systems frequently employ optical scanning as a means of capturing data.

Pre-printed data The entry of specified, recurring or fixed information on an OCR form at the time of manufacture.

Preprinted form A type of document on which preprinted information may be present. The fields are fixed and line spacing need not be constant.

Press Any device used to perform printing. Presses may be described by their capability (as a two color press), by their printing process (as an offset lighographic press), or by their mechanics (as a flat-bed press, cylinder press, platen press, or rotary press) or paper handling capability (sheet-fed press, roll-to-sheet press, roll-to-roll press).

Pressure sensitive Adhesive coating material on a carrier or backing sheet which when removed, will stick to another object with moistening. Often used in label production.

Print area That position of a form in which printed data may be placed for machine sensing (See clear area).

Print-contrast ratio See 'print contrast signal'.

Print Contrast Ratio (PCR) The ratio obtained by subtracting the reflectance at a data image from the maximum reflectance found within a specified distance from that area, and dividing the result by that maximum reflectance. Shown as (PCR).

Print Contrast Signal (PCS) A measure of the contrast between a printed character and the paper on which the character is printed. Shown as (PCS).

Print quality The inter-relationship of printed material and imprinted material that affects the optimum performance of the scanner.

Proof Positive print usually made from a negative to provide (1) an indication of the appearance of the final printed form, (2) to check composition accuracy and for client approval prior to production.

Rag content The amount of rag (usually cotton or linen fiber) used in manufacturing paper. In an optical reader, zero rag content is desirable.

Raster type scanning The method whereby the image is produced on a screen of luminescent material at an end of a cathode ray tube, or kinescope.

Read Mechanical interpretation of printed characters or marks. See scan.

Read area See 'print area'.

Read color (ink) Any markings to which an optical device is sensitive. See 'non reflective color (ink)' & 'scan color (ink)'.

Reading accuracy The ability of optical equipment to accurately read valid data.

Reading lens The device which focuses the images reflected from the form on the scanner. This lens is usually used to magnify the reflected image size.

Read/Sorter It will read and sort intermixed documents of various lengths, widths and thicknesses. The equipment is designed to read and translate the various data. The sorter can operate under control of the processor and is programmed to sort encoded items on a whole number of block basis in any desired order. Images are read and transferred directly to the memory of the processor. The documents read may be of intermixed size and thickness as is typically encountered in check handling operations. The standard minimum length of the document is 6 inches. Readers differ mainly in document reading rates. Type and speeds range from 950 to 2,000 documents per minute.

Read station The area in an optical system where reading is effected.

Read zone That portion of a document or sheet where printed information to be read by a reader may be placed.

Ream A specified quantity of paper, usually 500 sheets of specific sheet size. The U. S. Federal Government uses 1000 sheets.

Recognition system That part of a system that determines the identity of the image being scanned so as to generate a valid output code for computer use.

Record A collection of related items of data treated as a unit, usually consisting of one or more fields.

Reference edge That edge of a form which is used for alignment so that the printed data will be parallel to the direction of scanning. Same as alignment edge.

Reference mark A preprinted indicator on a document used as a base location point by a reading device. Also known as a registration mark.

Reflectance = R The measured level of light energy reflected by a paper substrate or imprinted characters thereon, expressed in percent of a standard reference material.

Reflectance diffuse Reflected light whose angle of reflection varies from the angle of incidence of the illuminating light, such as in reflection from a rough surface.

Reflective color (ink) See 'non-read color (ink)', 'blind color (ink)', & 'non scan color (ink)'.

Registration Correct geometric positioning of the scannable data to important factors of the reader involved.

Registration mark See 'reference mark'.

Reject An image which has been scanned but not recognized.

Reject rate The number of rejects stated as a percentage of total items. Scanner items can be characters, marks, fields, document, pages, etc.

Rescan The ability of a reader to automatically re-read an unrecognizable image.

Response position The area designated to mark information on a mark read form.

Reverse A printing technique that utilizes the inked background to create a non-inked image. The image in reverse printing would usually be the color of the paper on which the background is being printed.

Right justified Data is right justified when the right hand digit or character occupies the right hand position of the space allotted for that data.

Rotary press Press in which the plate is wrapped around, or in the form of a cylinder. In common usage used to refer to presses used to produce unit sets and continuous forms. Rotary equipment may print direct or offset, and may be shipped, roll-to-fold, roll-to sheet, or roll-to-roll.

Row A horizontal arrangement of data or other expressions, contrasts with column.

Scan A search for graphics to be recognized by the recognition unit of the optical scanner and the conversion of the optical signal to an electrical signal.

Scan area See 'print area'.

Scan band An area across a form which is searched by a scanner in a single stroke or pass.

Scan color (ink) See 'read color (ink)', 'non reflective color (ink)'.

Scan speed The rate at which a scanner can search for information.

Scanner See OBR, OCR & OMR.

Scanning rate The rate at which images are scanned, usually in terms of characters per second.

Screen Technique used to create a tone effect to nonscan printed images, which cause a dot pattern to be created. Screened images are defined in terms of line (e.g., 100 line screen may be 100 lines to the inch) and percent (a 40% screen should have an image in which 40% of the surface is inked).

Self-checking number or digit Value or digit associated with a number or numeric field (usually suffixed) which is used for automatic checking for errors in transcription, transmission, or in reading into the system. Weighted numbers and simple arithmetic systems are used. Also called modulus numbers or check numbers (specific systems are named modulus-7, modulus-9, modulus-11, or check-7, check-9, or mod-9, mod-11, etc.)

Serial numbering The assignment of sequential numbers to documents, usually under program control to assure against loss in processing.

Serif The short cross-lines at the end of the main strokes in Roman type faces.

Shelf Life The storage period which forms can be kept prior to utilization.

Shift register A matrix of electronic flip flops used to temporarily store the quantized video before recognition.

Show through The condition where printing on one side of the paper can be seen from the other side.

Skew With respect to printing, it is the rotational deviation of the printed image from its intended orientation relative to the document reference edge.

2. With respect to paper transport, it is the rotational deviation of the document from its intended position on the feed belt.

Skew tolerance The allowable angular displacement.

Smoothness A measure of document's surface resistance to airflow. As the resistance decreases, the smoothness number increases. Low paper smoothness is a desirable quality in optical scanning applications.

Smudges Dirty streaks or smears that may confuse the scanner, caused from slippage in a data entry device, mishandling of the form, care less storage, etc.

Source document A document which is entered directly into the optical equipment when received from the user with little or no processing.

Space A graphic shape which is a completely blank area.

Spacing See 'character spacing'.

Spectral response The variation in sensitivity of a device to light of different wavelengths.

Spots Areas outside the character outline limit which are contrasting with the background.

Stacker A device for accumulating processed documents in optical scanners and card readers.

Standard The ANSI Standard ;XX3.17-1974, 'character set for optical character recognition.' Defines the character shapes for OCR-A font.

Step An increment of a document or form being processed.

Stiffness The stiffness of paper is a measure of its ability to support its own weight.

Stock form Any 'off-the-shelf' form delivered to the user without further printing or other manufacturing operations. Also a form which is not necessarily 'off-the-shelf,' but which adheres to predetermined specifications in all respects.

2. Stock continuous may be blank or pre-printed with guide rules or screened bars.

Stroke A straight line or curve between two nodes of a character. Each character is made up of a variable number of these strokes. Their shape and arrangement define each individual character of a set. For a character to be read correctly, the quality of printing of each stroke must fall within certain tolerance limits. These limits are usually expressed in terms of stroke width.

Stroke analysis This scanning technique is based on the stroke or line formation for each character. The characters are differentiated from each other by the number and position of vertical and horizontal strokes. The formation of the unknown character is matched by a special purpose computer against a character truth table, which indicates the stroke information for each reference character.

Stub Fastened portion of a unit set, separated by means of a perforation, which when removed usually extracts the carbon paper as well; stubs are described by their orientation with the printed image (top stub, bottom stub, side stub) or by the way they enter the forms writing machine (leading stub, trailing stub); see also double stub, primary stub, drop stub.
2. Any portion of the form torn off during its use; also tear off.

Substitution A character or mark that is incorrectly recognized as another character or mark in the output machine signal.

Substitution rate The number of substitutions per given number of characters read expressed as a percent.

TAPPI Technical Association of the Pulp and Paper Industry, New York, New York. This group has developed standard methods to measure and compare the physical characteristics and performance of papers.

Terminal In data communications, any point in a network where data can enter or leave; more specifically, a device used to generate and transmit data or receive and record data. A printer and forms may or may not be involved.

Thermal printer Type of small non-impact printer which uses special paper coated or impregnated with material which reacts to heat applied by small electrical resistance elements to form a dot matrix image.

Thickness See 'caliper'.

Throughput The rate of processing documents or pages per minute through an optical system, usually expressed in forms per minute.

Timing mark A printed indicator along the edge of some OCR forms used to synchronize the form position with machine-scan cycles.

Timing track A series of timing marks in a track on which a pattern of signals is recorded to provide a timing reference.

Tolerance Permissible degree of variation from a preset standard.

Transmitted light scanner An optical scanner that operates by sensing light transmitted through paper instead of reflected from its surface.

Transparent inks Inks which permit previous printing on the paper substrate to show through and which are usually blind.

Transport The mechanical component of an optical device used to transport forms through the device, from input to output hoppers.

Turnaround document A form produced by an EDP system intended for future re-entry, possibly with added data, via an optical scanner.

Type and scan An optical scanning application in which input data having an unsuitable format or quality is retyped on machine readable forms.

Typefont Identity of graphic style according to the characteristics of shape.

Ultraviolet response A scanning system which reacts to light in the extreme blue region of the visual color spectrum.

Universal product code A specialized bar code developed by the grocery industry to allow scanner-equipped checkout terminals to capture product information optically.

Unit set A form which is provided with a multiply assembly attached by one or more edges to assure registration of plies during data entry. Such forms are single units as contrasted to continuous forms.

Upper case The large character, or capital letters, in a type font, as distinguished from the lower case characters or small letters.

Variable data Information entered on the form during the course of its use (as opposed to constant data, preprinted data).

Verify To check, usually with an automatic technique, to minimize the number of human errors or mistakes in the data transcription.

2. To make certain that the data prepared for the computer is correct.

Vertical field separators A vertical line separating data fields.

Visible response A particular type of optical response system used in some scanners. There are very few reflective inks for this type system.

Vocabulary The characters and fonts that a particular optical device is capable of recognizing.

Void The inadvertent absence of ink within an image outline usually resulting in degraded readability.

Wand scanner A hand-held optical scanner used in applications where it's impractical to transport data past a fixed read head.

Web A roll of paper used in web or rotary printing.

White standard A substance that reflects 100% light and is used in calibrating test instruments. See barium sulfate.

Width The distance between the two edges of a form, measured along a nominal data line as the form is fed through an optical reader.

Wire side The side of a paper sheet next to the wire carrier in the manufacturing process; opposite from the felt side (See felt side).

Word processing Computer assisted or automated preparation of office correspondence, reports, and other documents using systems that incorporate automatic typewriters, keyboard printers, and sometimes display equipment such as CRT's.

Write test Preliminary run of a proposed new form through the writing machine which will execute the final forms, normally to check image legibility.

Zero balance An effective method of data verification when both detail items and their summary are processed together. Each detail item is accumulated minus and the summary plus. The result is zero balance if both are correct.

Zero suppression The elimination of the zeros to the left of the significant digits, usually after reading.

Appendix B

An OCR Chronology

Early 1800's— Initial patents issued in U.S. for reading aids for the blind.

1870— C. Carey of Boston, Mass., researched image transmission device which used a mosaic of photocells.

1890— P. Nipkow of Poland developed sequential scanning ("Nipkow Disk").

1912— OCR patents for telegraphy applications issued to E. Goldberg in Chicago.

1914— Fournier D'Albe invented a handheld reader for the blind ("Optophone").

1928— Patent issued to E. Goldberg for his statistical machine.

1929— Patent issued to G. Tauschek for a reading machine.

1931— Patent issued to R. D. Parker and A. Weaver for telegraph reading devices.

1933— Patent issued to P. W. Handel for a statistical machine.

1938— Patent issued to W. Ayres for a "Light Sensitive Device".

1946— First published report on RCA's reading devices for the blind.

1950— Patents issued to E. Davis and O. Hinton, Jr., for an ''Apparatus for the Reading of Facsimile and Printed Matter By the Blind''.

1950-51— D. Shepherd built and demonstrated his ''GISMO'' reading machine.

1951— D. Shepherd established Intelligent Machines Research (IMR) Corporation.

1952— J. Rabinow built first DOFL reading machine in collaboration with the National Bureau of Standards.

1953— Patent issued to D. Shepherd for an ''Apparatus for Reading''.

1953— M. M. Levy developed reading machines for use in mail-sorting operations for the Post Office of Canada.

1954— Farrington purchased first ''Scandex'' equipment from IMR.

1954— M. L. Greenough and C. C. Gordon demonstrated their reader for typewritten characters at the National Bureau of Standards.

1956— IMR equipment for scanning petroleum charge cards sold to Farrington, then leased to Standard Oil of California for use in Salt Lake City.

1956— IMR installed first true OCR reading machine at Reader's Digest, Pleasantville, New York.

1956— IMR licensed D. Shepherd's inventions to IBM.

1956— American Bankers Association recommended adoption of magnetic ink for high-speed machine automatic character recognition.

1956— Bell Laboratories demonstrated the "STYLATOR", a stylus recording device for reading numerical hand-printing by toll operators.

1959— First page reader installed by IMR for use by United States Air Force.

1959— First analyzing reader built by IMR for U.S. Post Office.

1959— IMR and Farrington merged manufacturing operations (Farrington Purchases IMR).

Late 1950's— Industry wide improvements to forms, specifications, paper, inks, and printing to improve OCR read rates.

1960's and later— Companies such as Standard Register, Moore, UARCO, and Burroughs were instrumental in helping to establish the standardization of OCR fonts, inks, and papers in conjunction with ANSI committees.

1960— National Data Processing Company of Dallas installed first optical scanning system built to handle retail accounts receivable.

1960— Philco Corporation's Research Division developed an all-electronic alpha-number recognition device for identifying typed or printed envelope addresses for U.S. Post Office.

1960— ANSI X3A1 committee on automatic data processing established.

1961— IBM announced 141B, OCR Document Reader.

1961— National Cash Register (NCR) installed first journal tape reader.

1961— Long-range program in OCR pattern and character recognition initiated at General Motors Research Laboratories, Warren, Michigan.

1961— Rabinow Engineering Company Laboratories demonstrated a machine for reading handwritten numerals—Ryder installation.

1961— IBM displayed an experimental constrained handwritten character recognizer at the Western Joint Computer Conference.

1961— Recognition Equipment Incorporated (REI) founded by Herman Philipson in Dallas, Texas.

1961— REI announced first practical, high-speed retina scanner ("Electronic Retina").

1964— IBM introduced 1282, Document Card Reader.

1964— REI installed first OCR airline ticket reader at United Airlines in Chicago.

1964— REI installed first multi-font reader at Fireman's Fund Insurance, San Francisco ("RIPC").

1964— Control Data Corporation (CDC) acquired Rabinow Engineering Company.

1964— NCR Corporation released the NCR 420 journal tape reader to read cash register tapes.

1965— REI installed first OCR equipment for use in printing/publishing industry at Perry Publications.

1965— First CDC "915" installed.

1965— Michigan installs OCR equipment at state offices, first such installation by a state government.

Mid 1960's— Introduction of the first "reflectometer" that could be used in a production printing environment.

1966— IBM installed first "1287" document reader.

1966— Business Equipment Manufacturing Association (BEMA) proposed adoption of OCR-A font—subsequently adopted by National Standards Institute.

1966— European "GIRO's" installed initial OCR equipment and European manufacturers adopted OCR-B font.

1967— Cognitronics introduced "Remote Optical Character Recognition".

1967— American Express was first credit card company to install OCR equipment.

1967— REI installed first integrated OCR/ink-jet printing equipment at oil companies.

1967— Scan-Data installed initial "250" OCR reader.

1968— Remote OCR applications announced and demonstrated by REI.

1968— REI delivered the first high-speed OCR document transport to oil companies.

1968— Scan Optics incorporated in Sept. 1968.

1969— Scan-Data machines read numeric handprint.

1970— OCR User's Association established in Houston, Texas.

1971— IBM installed first 1288, page reader.

1970— REI shipped first high-speed multi-font OCR system to United States Postal Service.

1970— REI shipped initial "Input 80" system to Japan.

1970— Introduction of the Scan-Optics System 20/20.

1970— Scan-Data introduced SWAMI the first Heuristic software recognition capability.

1971— Scan-Data introduced a multi-font read capability..

1971— Office Business Machines (OBM) introduced the "Laser 1," a vacuum feed laser scanner.

1972— REI sold its first TRACE system, to be used for bank check processing at rates of up to 2400 checks per minute.

1972— Taplin Business Machines founded. Read miniature bar codes printed by special typeballs.

1972— Scan-Data introduced the Scan-Flex, 2250/1, OCR System.

1973— Scan-Data introduced the 2250/2 Key entry system and the 2250/3 mixed media system.

1973— General Instrument installed first Documate system developed by its electronic systems division.

1973— Hendrix introduced a OCR-1 reader.

1973— BancTec introduced the Checkmender I and Heatstrip.

1973— Introduction of the Scan-Optics System 20/10.

1973— IBM introduced the "3886-1" and "-2", on-line, friction-feed, LED scanners featuring recognition units.

1973— REI developed the prototype models of the OCR WAND handheld readers.

1974— Cummins-Allison introduced the "SCANAK 4216", equipment having a scanner, photo-cells, matrix recognition unit, friction-feed; on-line to "Key-Scan".

1974—75 Scan-Data machines accommodated alphabetic handprint and enter-mixed alphanumeric handprint.

1975— Introduction of the Scan-Optics Systems 530, 540, and the stand alone system 501.

1975— Hendrix introduced a OCR-2 reader.

1975— REI shipped first "LIPAP" OCR postal automation system to France.

1975— Scan-Optics "540" introduced; system including microfilmer, vacuum-feed, image directions; on-line to "Scan-Edit".

1976— Hendrix introduced a Typereader 1.

1976— BancTec introduced the Basic Off-Line Core System (Computerized Optical Reader & Encoder).

1976— Introduction of the Scan-Optics Scan Edit systems 300, 600, and 3500.

1976— Scan-Data introduced a continuous feed mechanism.

1977— Scan-Data introduced POSITRAN point of sale system.

1977— Recognition Business Systems (REI subsidiary) introduced MAPS system, high-speed, automatic ZIP code sorting system.

1977— REI announced "Input 80 C1" page reader; friction-feed, linear array, matrix feature recognition unit, on-line to "Total Data Entry (TDE)" system.

1977— Scan-Optics introduced "506" equipment; off-line, linear array, feature analysis, work station-video collect system.

1977— BanTec introduced the On-Line Core System and Advanced MICR Reject Processor.

1977— IBM announced 3895, Handprint Reader from Checks.

1978— BancTec introduced Checkmender II.

1978— Scan-Data/Control Data affiliation.

1978— Hendrix introduced an Underline Processing Option for TYPE-READER 1 and 2.

1978— REI introduced "3400" line of portable OCR WAND Reader terminals.

1978— REI announced a "Currency Verification and Counting System (CVCS)"; for processing bank notes at Federal Reserve System locations, at rates of up to 72,000 notes per hour.

1978— Hendrix introduced a Single line spacing and dual pitch options on TYPEREADER 1.

1978— Hendrix introduced a TYPEREADER 2.

1979— Introduction of the Scan-Optics system 2500.

1979— REI introduced "TRACE IMAGE System (TRIM)", coupling OCR with image processing technology; to be used by banks for check truncation.

1979— Burroughs entered OCR market with purchase of Context Corporation.

1979— Hendrix introduced a TELE-TYPEREADER message entry system to International Market.

1979— Bell and Howell introduced S-IV mail sorter.

1979— BancTec introduced a Credit Card Processing System.

1980— REI listed on New York Stock Exchange.

1980— BancTec introduced a Multi-Transport System. BancTec introduced a Return Item Processing Software.

1980— Hendrix introduced a TYPEREADER TR3.

1980— Hendrix introduced a TYPEREADER TR2S.

1980— Cognitronics introduced the OCR/800 series.

1980— Bell and Howell introduced S-III sorter and Manual data entry machine.

1980— Hendrix introduced a TELE-TYPEREADER System to U.S. Market.

Appendix C
References

Baasch, Thomas L. "Optical Character Recognition." Published in the February, 1970 issue of "Electronic Products."

Barber, Richard D. "Application of Optical Character Recognition in Tomorrow's Office."

Braunbeck, J. "Optical Character Recognition." Published in the May/June, 1972 issue of "Information Display."

Chu, Albert L. G. "The Plodding Progress of OCR."

Dunn, Nina L. "The Office of the Future." Published in the July and August, 1979 issues of "Computer Designs."

Freedman, M. D. "Optical Character Recognition." Published in the March, 1974 issue of "IEEE Spectrum."

Geremedhin, Elinor. "Optical Character Recognition—Performance Up, Prices Down." Published in the June, 1970 issue of "Data Processing Magazine."

Gray, Peter J. "An OCR Chronology."

Hansen, John R. "OCR Joins the Team." Published in the July, 1978 issue of "Infosystems."

Lasden, Martin, "A Painless Boost in Productivity." Published in the December, 1979 issue of "Computer Decisions."

Lusa, John M. "The Computer in Our lives." Published in the January, 1980 issue of "Infosystems."

Nadler, Morton. "The State of the Art in OCR—1972."

National Retail Merchants Association. "NRMA/OCR-A—Cost/Benefit Study."

Newman, E. A. "Character Recognition—The Way Ahead." Published in the March, 1967 issue of "Electronics and Power."

"The Office of the Future." A special report published in the August, 1979 issue of "Dun's Review."

Poitevent, J. L. "OCR for Credit Card Processing." Published in the July, 1969 issue of "Datamation."

Rabinow, David. "Recent Developments in OCR." Published in the May/June, 1970 issue of "Data Processing."

Rabinow, Jacob C. "Sense and Nonsense, or Pride and Prejudice in the Design of Characters for Optical Character Recognition."

Rabinow, Jacob C. "Whither OCR?" Published in the July, 1969 issue of Datamation."

Reagan, Fonnie H., Jr. "Should OCR Be Your Data Input Medium?" Published in June, 1971.

Rhodes, Wayne L. "Breaking the Stranglehold." Published in the July, 1979 issue of "Infosystems."

Rhodes, Wayne, L. "The Office of the Future." Published in the March, 1980 issue of "Infosystems."

Schantz, Herbert F. "Increased Productivity Through the Use of OCR Data Entry Systems." Published by Recognition Equipment Incorporated in October, 1978.

Schantz, Herbert F. "Optical Character Recognition—The Impact of a Maturing Technology on Future User Applications." Published in the November, 1977 issue of "OCR Today."

Schantz, Herbert F. "Optical Character Recognition: The Key to Increased Productivity in Data Entry for Yesterday, Today and Tomorrow." Published by Recognition Equipment Incorporated in October, 1979.

Schantz, Herbert F. "Optical Character Recognition Technology—The Machines That Read to Computers." Published in the November, 1978 issue of "OCR Today."

Schantz, Herbert F. "Optrical Character Recognition—Proven Technology for Increased Productivity of Data Entry Systems." Published by Recognition Equipment Incorporated in October, 1978.

Schantz, Herbert F. "OCR: Tying Taproot Technology Into Data Entry Productivity." Published in the December, 1979 issue of "Data Management."

Sheinberg, Israel. "Optical Character Recognition for Information Management." Published as part of a compendium of OCR reports by Thompson Book Company, 1968.

Stevens, Mary Elizabeth. "Automatic Character Recognition—A State-of-the-Art Report." Published by the National Bureau of Standards, United States Department of Commerce, May, 1961.

Strelau, Conrad A. and Schantz, Herbert F. "The Evolution of OCR Equipment in Total Data Entry Systems." Published in the April, 1977 issue of "OCR Today."

Strelau, Conrad A. and Schantz, Herbert F. "Optical Character Recognition Equipment." Published in the June, 1975 issue of "The Office."

Stepke, Edwin. "OCR: Scanning For The Future." Published in the December, 1972 issue of "Electro-Optical Systems Design."

Talbot, J. E. "The Human Side of Data Input." Published in the April, 1971 issue of "Data Processing Management."

The Texas Giants. Published in 1970 by the Texas Industrial Commission. Withington, Frederick G. "Beyond 1984: A Technology Forecast." Published in the January, 1975 issue of "Datamation."

Guide to Footnotes

1. H. F. Schantz, "OCR: The Key to Increased Productivity in Data Entry for Yesterday, Today and Tomorrow"
2. ibid
3. ibid
4. J. Rabinow, "Sense and Nonsense," page 3
5. Schantz
6. Rabinow, pp. 3–4
7. ibid, p. 4
8. ibid, pp. 4–5
9. J. Rabinow, "Whither OCR?"
10. Schantz
11. ibid
12. Rabinow, "Sense and Nonsense," page 8
13. ibid, pp. 10–11
14. Schantz
15. ibid
16. *The Texas Giants,* page 36
17. ibid, p. 37
18. Schantz
19. *The Texas Giants,* page 37
20. ibid, p. 38
21. Schantz
22. ibid
23. ibid
24. ibid
25. E. Geremedhin, "OCR: Performance Up, Prices Down"

26. Schantz
27. Rabinow, "Whither OCR?"
28. Geremedhin
29. ibid
30. ibid
31. ibid
32. ibid
33. Schantz
34. Geremedhin
35. Rabinow, "Whither OCR?"
36. ibid
37. Schantz
38. P. Gray, "An OCR Chronology."
39. *The Texas Giants,* pp 39–40
40. ibid, pp 42–43
41. A. Keller, "Infosystems," February, 1980, page 32
42. ibid
43. H. Schantz, Presentation for 1979 DEMA Conference
44. "P. R. Reporter," August 20, 1979, page 3
45. J. R. Reese, Keynote Address to 1980 Winter OCRUA Conference
46. "Computerworld," May 5, 1980, page 8

Index

Accordion Fold, 67 Appendix A
Accumulator, 67 Appendix A
Accuracy, 67 Appendix A
Addressograph-Multigraph, 15, 36
Addressograph Plastic Credit Card, 16
Adjacent Characters, 67 Appendix A
Airline Tickets, 42
Airline Ticket Reader, 96 Appendix B
Alignment Edge, 67 Appendix A
Alpha Character, 67 Appendix A
Alpha/Numeric Characters, 67 Appendix A
American Bankers Association, 13, 94 Appendix B
American Express Company 28, 97 Appendix B
American National Standards Institute, 37
American Standards Institute (ANSI), 19, 68 Appendix A
American Telephone and Telegraph Company (AT&T), 3, 16
Angstrom, 67 Appendix A
ANSI, 95 Appendix B
ANSI Subcommittee X3A1, 68 Appendix A, 95, Appendix B
Apparatus for Reading, 9, 94 Appendix B
Application, 68 Appendix A
Arizona Public Service Company, 16, 19

Armed Forces, 17
Array, 68 Appendix A
Ascender, 68 Appendix A
Aspect Ratio, 68 Appendix A
Atlantic City Electric Company, 16
Audible Narration, 43
Audible Tone, 8
Ayres, Waldemar, 5, 93 Appendix B

Back Printing, 68 Appendix A
Background Color (Ink), 68 Appendix A
Background Reflectance, 68 Appendix A
Backspace, 68 Appendix A
Bad Ribbons, 48
BancTec, 98 Appendix B, 99 Appendix B, 100 Appendix B
Bank of America, 33
Bar Code, 45, 68 Appendix A
Bar Code Printer, 68 Appendix A
Bar-Code Reader, 36, 68 Appendix A
Bar Code Reader Sorter, 68 Appendix A
Bar Printer, 69 Appendix A
Bard of Avon, 44
Barium Sulphate, 68 Appendix A
Bark Mark, 69 Appendix A
Base Line, 69 Appendix A
Basis Weight (Paper), 69 Appendix A
Batch, 69 Appendix A

Batch Processing, 69 Appendix A
Batch Total, 69 Appendix A
Bell and Howell, 100 Appendix B
Bell Laboratories, 12, 95 Appendix B
BEMA, 97 Appendix B
Bent Keys, 48
Binary, 69 Appendix A
Binary Coded Decimal (BCD), 69 Appendix A
Bit, 69 Appendix A
Blank Space, 69 Appendix A
Blind, 43, 93 Appendix B
Blink Color (Ink), 69 Appendix A
Block, 69 Appendix A
Body (Ink), 70 Appendix A
Bolger, William F., 65
Braille, Louis, 5
Brightness, 70 Appendix A
Bulk (Paper), Page 70 Appendix A
Burroughs, 13, 17, 56, 100 Appendix B
Burst, 70 Appendix A
Burster, 70 Appendix A
Bush's, Dr. Vannevar 'Rapid Selector', 10
Business Equipment Manufacturers Association (BEMA), 37
Business Form, 70 Appendix A
Bytes, 62, 70 Appendix A

Caliper Paper, 70 Appendix A
Cancel Character, 70 Appendix A
Carbon, 70 Appendix A
Carbon Black, 70 Appendix A
Carbon Paper, 70 Appendix A
Carbonized Paper, 70 Appendix A
Carbonless Paper, 70 Appendix A
Card Set, 71 Appendix A
Carey, C. R., 1, 93 Appendix B
Carriage Return (CR), 71 Appendix A
Cathode Ray Tube Display (CRT Display), 71 Appendix A
CBEMA, 71 Appendix A
Centerline Stroke (Character), 71 Appendix A
Central Processing Unit (CPU), 71 Appendix A
Ceral Boxes, 42
Chain Printer, 71 Appendix A
Character, 45, 71 Appendix A
Character Alignment, 70 Appendix A
Character Boundry, 71 Appendix A
Character Density, 71 Appendix A

Character Dimensions, 72 Appendix A
Character Erase, 71 Appendix A
Character Misread, 70 Appendix A
Character Outline, 71 Appendix A
Character Reader, 72 Appendix A
Character Recognition, 72 Appendix A
Character Set, 72 Appendix A
Character Skew, 72 Appendix A
Character Spacing, 72 Appendix A
Character Stroke Width, 72 Appendix A
Character Style (Font), 72 Appendix A
Check Digit, 72 Appendix A
Civil Service Commission, 17
Cleanliness, 72 Appendix A
Clear Area, 72 Appendix A
Clock Mark, 72 Appendix A
Clock Track, 72 Appendix A
Cluneve Type, 21
Cognitronics Company, 33, 34, 35, 56, 97 Appendix B, 100 Appendix B
Collate, 72 Appendix A
Collator, 72 Appendix A
Color, 73 Appendix A
Column, 73 Appendix A
Column-Arranged Photocells, 47
Compile, 73 Appendix A
Composition, 73 Appendix A
CompuScan and Information International, 35
Consecutive Numbering, 73 Appendix A
Constraint Boxes, 73 Appendix A
Context Corporation, 100 Appendix B
Continuous Form, 73 Appendix A
Contrast, 73 Appendix A
Control Data Corporation, 11, 21, 25, 31, 32, 33, 34, 56, 96 Appendix B
Control Character, 73 Appendix A
Control Instruments Company, 13
Control Panel, 72 Appendix A
Control Total, 73 Appendix A
Controlled Cathode Ray Tube Beams, 47
Controller, 73 Appendix A
Convert, 73 Appendix A
Cook, Harvey, 8
Coordinates, 73 Appendix A
Copy, 73 Appendix A
Corner Cut, 73 Appendix A
Counter, 73 Appendix A
Crash Imprinting, 74 Appendix A

Credit Card Charge Tickets, 28
Crocker Citizens National Bank, 32
Crossfooting, 73 Appendix A
CRT, 35, 71 Appendix A
Cummins-Allison, 98 Appendix B
Currency Verification and Counting System (CVCS), 100 Appendix B
Curve Tracing or Following, 74 Appendix A
Custom Form, 74 Appendix A
Cut Sheet, 74 Appendix A

D'Albe, Edmund Fournier, 2, 94 Appendix B
Dallas Chamber of Commerce, 24
Dallas Market Center, 29
Data, 74 Appendix A
Data Collection, 74 Appendix A
Data Correction Features, 51
Data Entry, 4, 42
Data Entry Awareness Report, 54, 55
Data Field, 74 Appendix A
Data Lifting, 45
Data Manipulation, 42
Data Processing Magazine, 31
Datamation, 33
Davis, E., 94 Appendix B
Davies, Fred, 23, 25
Debug, 74 Appendix A
Decollator, 74 Appendix A
Deleaver, 74 Appendix A
Delete Character, 74 Appendix A
Delimiter, 74 Appendix A
Descender, 74 Appendix A
De-Skewing Fingers, 74 Appendix A
Detection Component, 45
Detection Scanning Modes, 47
Detection Section, 45
Diamond Ordnance Fuze Laboratories (DOFL), 10, 94 Appendix B
Diffuse Reflectance, 74 Appendix A
Digit, 74 Appendix A
Digital Memory Improvements, 47
Dirt, 75 Appendix A
Disk Flipper, 28
Document, 75 Appendix A
Document Card Reader, 96 Appendix B
Document Reader, 74 Appendix A, 97 Appendix B
Document Reference Edge, 75 Appendix A

Document Registration Time, 75 Appendix A
DOT Matrix Printer, 75 Appendix A
Couble Correlation, 35
Double Detector, 75 Appendix A
Double Document Detection, 75 Appendix A
Double Face Carbon, 75 Appendix A
Drier, 75 Appendix A
Drop-out Colors (Ink), 75 Appendix A
Drum Printer, 75 Appendix A
Dry Offset, 75 Appendix A

Eads, Jessica, 23, 25
ECMA, 75 Appendix A
Edge, 75 Appendix A
Edit, 75 Appendix A
EDP, 76 Appendix A
Electric Pencil, 6
Electric Typewriter, 76 Appendix A
Electronic Retina, 25, 26, 27, 96 Appendix B
Electronic Retina Computing Reader (ERCR), 25, 27, 59
Elite, 76 Appendix A
Embossing, 76 Appendix A
Encode, 76 Appendix A
Encoder, 76 Appendix A
Erase Character, 76 Appendix A
Error Rate, 76 Appendix A
Escort Memory, 42
Extraneous Ink, 76 Appendix A
EYE, 15

Face, 76 Appendix A
Fanfold, 76 Appendix A
Farrington, 94 Appendix B
Farrington Electronics, 15
Farrington Manufacturing, 11, 17, 19, 25, 31, 34, 36
Fastening, 76 Appendix A
Feature Analysis, 50
Feed Belt, 76 Appendix A
Feed Wheels, 76 Appendix A
Felt Side, 76 Appendix A
Fiberopic Digital Cables, 64
Field, 77 Appendix A
Field Mark, 77 Appendix A
Field-Prepared Form, 77 Appendix A
Field-Separator Mark, 77 Appendix A
File Hold Punching, 77 Appendix A

Fireman's Fund Insurance Company, 27, 96 Appendix B
First National City Bank, 16, 59
Flow, 77 Appendix A
Flow Chart, 77 Appendix A
Fluorescence, 77 Appendix A
Flying Spot, 47
Flying Spot Scanner, 77 Appendix A
Font, 77 Appendix A
Form, 77 Appendix A
Format, 77 Appendix A
Format Identifier, 77 Appendix A
Forms Analysis, 77 Appendix A
Forms Control, 77 Appendix A
Forms Design, 78 Appendix A
Forms Handling Equipment, 78 Appendix A
Framing, 78 Appendix A
Free Form, 78 Appendix A
Full Matrix Scan, 78 Appendix A
Fuzz, 78 Appendix A

General Electric (GE), 15
General Instrument, 98 Appendix B
General Motors Research Laboratories, 96 Appendix B
General Motors Technical Center, 21
Generic Composition, 56
GIRO'S, 97 Appendix B
GISMO, 8, 94 Appendix B
Gloss, 78 Appendix A
Goldberg, Emmanuel, 2, 4, 93 Appendix B, 94 Appendix B
Gordon, C. C., 12, 94 Appendix B
Grain Direction, 78 Appendix A
Graphic, 78 Appendix A
Greenough, M. L., 12, 94 Appendix B
Grid, 78 Appendix A
Groundwood Paper, 78 Appendix A
Group Erase, 78 Appendix A
Guard Bank, 78 Appendix A
Guide Boxes, 78 Appendix A
Guide Edge, 78 Appendix A

Handel, P. W., 4, 93 Appendix B
Handel, Paul H., 4
Handheld Reader, 59, 98 Appendix B
Handprint, 78 Appendix A
Handprint Boxes 78 Appendix A
Head Margin, 79 Appendix A
Header, 79 Appendix A

Hendrix, 98 Appendix B, 99 Appendix B, 100 Appendix B
Heuristic Software Recognition Capability, 97 Appendix B
High Speed Mirror, 79 Appendix A
Hinton, O. Jr., 94 Appendix B
Hollerith Punch Card, 44
Horizontal Spacing, 79 Appendix A
Hot Spot Carbonizing, 79 Appendix A
Hughes Aircraft, 25

Illegal Character, 79 Appendix A
Image, 79 Appendix A
Image Dissector, 79 Appendix A
Impact Printer, 79 Appendix A
Imprinters, 48, 79 Appendix A
Imprinting, 79 Appendix A
Information International, 36
Infosystems, 16
Infrared Response (IR), 79 Appendix A
Ink Bleed, 79 Appendix A
Ink-Jet Printer (IJP), 29, 79 Appendix A
Ink-Jet Printing, 97 Appendix B
Ink Smudge, 79 Appendix A
Input Bottleneck, 62
Input Device-Optical Reader, 79 Appendix A
Integrated Retina, 57
Intelligent Machines Research Corporation (IMR), 9, 11, 15, 94 Appendix B, 95 Appendix B
International Business Machines Corporation (IBM), 5, 15, 19, 21, 25, 31, 33, 34, 56, 95 Appendix B, 96 Appendix B, 97 Appendix B, 98 Appendix B, 99 Appendix B
IOS, 79 Appendix A
ISO-B, 38

Journal Tape, 80 Appendix A
Journal Tape Feed Options, 36
Journal Tape Reader, 21, 95 Appendix B

Keller, Arnold, 16, 60
Key-to-Disk, 43
Key-to-Tape, 43
Keyboard, 80 Appendix A
Keyboard Arrangement, 80 Appendix A

Keyboard Layout, 80 Appendix A
Keyboard-to-Disc, 54
Keyboard-to-Tape, 54
Keypunch, 80 Appendix A
Keypunching, 57

Label, 80 Appendix A
Lasers, 47, 80 Appendix A
Laser Beams, 47
Laser Scanner, 80 Appendix A
Layout Sheet, 80 Appendix A
Leading Edge, 80 Appendix A
Left Justified, 80 Appendix A
Length, 80 Appendix A
Lens, 80 Appendix A
Letter Spacing, 80 Appendix A
Letterpress, 80 Appendix A
Levy, Maurice M., 12, 94 Appendix B
Light-Emitting Diodes, 47
Light Pipes, 80 Appendix A
Light Sensitive Device, 5
Line Boundary, 80 Appendix A
Line Holes, 80 Appendix A
Line Printer, 81 Appendix A
Line Separation, 81 Appendix A
Line Skew, 81 Appendix A
Line Spacing, 81 Appendix A
LIPAP, 99 Appendix B
Lithography, 81 Appendix A
Lockup Space, 81 Appendix A
Logic, 81 Appendix A
Logic Discrimination Sequence, 50
Long-Vertical Mark, 81 Appendix A
Lower Case, 81 Appendix A
LPM, 81 Appendix A
Lundberg, Eric, 56

Machine Readable, 81 Appendix A
Magnesium Oxide, 81 Appendix A
Magnetic Ink, 81 Appendix A
Magnetic Ink Character Recognition, 82
    Appendix A
Main Frame, 81 Appendix A
Management and Business Automa-
    tion, 15
Manifold, 81 Appendix A
Margin, 81 Appendix A
Mark, 45
Mark Read, 82 Appendix A
Mark Readers, 36
Marking Position, 82 Appendix A
Master Driving Record Central Files, 28

Matrix Matching, 82 Appendix A
Mechanical Disk Scanner, 82 Appendix
    A
Mechanical Self-Contained Paper, 82
    Appendix A
Mechanical Servoing, 82 Appendix A
Methods of Scanning, 10
Michigan State Government, 96 Ap-
    pendix B
MICR, 82 Appendix A
MIL, 82 Appendix A
Misaligned Carriages, 48
Misaligned Platens, 48
Montgomery Ward, 60
Moore, 56, 95 Appendix B
Mopper, 79 Appendix A
Morse Code, 2, 3, 8
Multi-Font Machine, 82 Appendix A
Multi-Web Press, 82 Appendix A
Multiple Font Machine, 82 Appendix A

Nanometer, 83 Appendix A
National Aeronautics Space Adminis-
    tration (NASA), 27
National Biscuit Company, 16
National Bureau of Standards, 10, 12,
    17, 94 Appendix B
National Cash Register (NCR), 15, 21,
    32, 36, 95 Appendix B, 96 Appendix
    B
National Data Processing Company, 15,
    19, 20, 23, 25, 95 Appendix B
National Standards Institute, 97 Appen-
    dix B
NDP 'Readatron', 15
Negative, 83 Appendix A
New York Stock Exchange, 28
Nipkow Disk, 2, 93 Appendix B
Nipkow, P., 2, 93 Appendix B
Noise, 83 Appendix A
Non-Freeze Carbon, 83 Appendix A
Non-Impact Printer, 83 Appendix A
Non-Read Color (Ink), 83 Appendix A
Non-Reflective Color (Ink), 83 Appen-
    dix A
Non Scan Color (Ink), 83 Appendix A
Numeric, 83 Appendix A
Nunley, Len, 25

OBM, 98 Appendix B
OBR, 83 Appendix A
OCR, 83 Appendix A

OCR 'A', 34, 38, 83 Appendix A, 97
    Appendix B
OCR-B Font, 38, 83 Appendix A, 97
    Appendix B
OCR Revisited, 54
OCR Wand, 47, 59, 98 Appendix B
Off-Line, 83 Appendix A
Offset Printing, 84 Appendix A
Ohio Bell Telephone, 16
Olsen, Jack, 8
Omnifont Reader, 36
OMR, 83 Appendix A
On-Line, 84 Appendix A
On-Line Output, 46
One-Time Carbon, 84 Appendix A
Opacity, 84 Appendix A
Opaque Ink, 84 Appendix A
Operation, 51
Optical, 84 Appendix A
Optical Bar Code Recognition, 84 Ap-
    pendix A
Optical Brightener, 84 Appendix A
Optical Character Recognition, 84 Ap-
    pendix A
Optical Character Recognition Users
    Association (OCRUA), 39, 54, 61, 64,
    97 Appendix B
Optical Mark Recognition, 84 Appen-
    dix A
Optical Path, 84 Appendix A
Optical Reader, 85 Appendix A
Optical Scanner, 84 Appendix A
Optical Scanning Corporation, 31
Optical Type Font, 84 Appendix A
Optic, 84 Appendix A
Optophone, 3, 93 Appendix B
Original, 84 Appendix A
Output Section, 45
Output Stackers, 84 Appendix A
Over Printing, 84 Appendix A

Page Reader, 85 Appendix A
Pantone Matching System (PMS), 85
    Appendix A
Paper Caliper, 85 Appendix A
Paper Grain, 85 Appendix A
Paper Reflectance, 85 Appendix A
Paper Smoothness, 85 Appendix A
Paper Transport, 47
Paper Weight, 85 Appendix A
Parker, R. D., 4, 93 Appendix B
Pattern Recognition, 85 Appendix A

Penny, J. C., 60
Perforation, 85 Appendix A
Perry, Gordon, 23
Philipson, Herman L., Jr., 20, 22, 23,
    24, 25, 31, 96 Appendix B
Philco, 32, 95 Appendix B
Philco-Ford, 17, 19, 33
Photocell Developments, 47
Photodiodes, 57
Photoelectric Cell, 85 Appendix A
Photomultiplier, 85 Appendix A
Pica, 85 Appendix A
Pinfeed, 85 Appendix A
Pitch, 85 Appendix A
Platen, 85 Appendix A
Porosity, 85 Appendix A
Pos, 85 Appendix A
POSITRAN, 99 Appendix B
Post Office of Canada, 12
Pre-Printed Data, 86 Appendix A
Preprinted Form, 85 Appendix A
Press, 86 Appendix A
Pressure Sensitive, 86 Appendix A
Print Area, 86 Appendix A
Print Contrast Ratio (PCR), 85 Appen-
    dix A, 86 Appendix A
Print Contrast Signal (PCS), 85 Appen-
    dix A, 86 Appendix A
Print Quality, 86 Appendix A
Printed Circuit Technology, 47
Proof, 86 Appendix A
Punched Card Formats, 8

Rabinow, Dr. Jacob C. (Jack), 5, 10,
    12, 13, 33, 34, 37, 94 Appendix B
Rabinow Engineering Company Labo-
    ratories 10, 21, 96 Appendix B, 98
    Appendix B, 99 Appendix B, 100 Ap-
    pendix B
Rabinow Engineering Division of Con-
    trol Data Corporation, 10, 17, 21
Radio Corporation of America's (RCA),
    5, 6, 15, 21, 32, 94 Appendix B
Rag Content, 86 Appendix A
Rapid Index Page Carrier (RIPC), 27
Raster Type Scanning, 86 Appendix A
Read, 86 Appendix A
Read Area, 86 Appendix A
Read Color (Ink), 86 Appendix A
Read/Sorter, 86 Appendix A
Read Station, 87 Appendix A
Read Zone, 87 Appendix A

Reader's Digest, 11, 16, 94 Appendix B
Reading Accuracy, 86 Appendix A
Reading Lens, 86 Appendix A
Real-World, 42
Ream, 87 Appendix A
Recognition, 48
Recognition Business Systems, 99 Appendix B
Recognition Equipment Incorporated (REI), 20, 22, 23, 25, 28, 29, 31, 32, 33, 56, 57, 58, 64
Recognition Section, 45
Recognition System, 87 Appendix A
Record, 87 Appendix A
Reese, Jay Rodney, 64
Reference Edge, 87 Appendix A
Reference Mark, 87 Appendix A
Reference Matrix, 50
Reflectance, 87 Appendix A
Reflectance Diffuse, 87 Appendix A
Reflective Color (Ink), 89 Appendix A
Registration, 87 Appendix A
Registration Mark, 87 Appendix A
Reject, 87 Appendix A
Reject Rate, 87 Appendix A
Reject Reentry, 43
Rejection Rates, 48
Remittance-Processing, 55
Remote Optical Character Recognition, 97 Appendix B
Remote Time-Sharing Retina, 29
Representatives of Europe's OCR Association (EUROCRA), 56
Rescan, 87 Appendix A
Research Institute of the National Retail Merchants Association, 13
Response Position, 88 Appendix A
Retina Scanner, 2
Reverse, 88 Appendix A
Right Justified, 88 Appendix A
RIPC, 28
Rotary Press, 88 Appendix A
Rotating Disks, 47
Row, 88 Appendix A
Ryder Installation, 96 Appendix B
Ryder Trucking Company, 21

Scan, 88 Appendix A
Scan Area, 88 Appendix A
Scan Band, 88 Appendix A
Scan Color (Ink), 88 Appendix A
Scan-Data, 33, 35, 56, 97 Appendix B, 98 Appendix B, 99 Appendix B
Scan Optics, 56, 97 Appendix B, 98 Appendix B, 99 Appendix B
Scan Speed, 88 Appendix A
Scandex, 12, 94 Appendix B
Scanner, 88 Appendix A
Scanning Rate, 88 Appendix A
Screen, 88 Appendix A
Search Plate, 4
Sears Roebuck, 60
Self-Checking Number or Digit, 88 Appendix A
Sense and Nonsense, 10
Serial Numbering, 88 Appendix A
Serif, 88 Appendix A
Sheinberg, Israel, 25
Shelf Lift, 88 Appendix A
Shepard, Dr. David, 8, 12, 33, 34, 94 Appendix B
Shift Register, 89 Appendix A
Show Through, 89 Appendix A
Significant Technological Products, 29
Six-Bit Binary Code, 5
Skew, 89 Appendix A
Skew Tolerance, 89 Appendix A
Smith, Barbara, 23, 25
Smithsonian Institute, 10
Smoothness, 89 Appendix A
Smudges, 89 Appendix A
Source Documents, 43, 89 Appendix A
Southwestern Medical School, 25
Space, 89 Appendix A
Spacing, 89 Appendix A
Spectral Response, 89 Appendix A
Sperry Rand Division of UNIVAC, 20
Spots, 89 Appendix A
Stacker, 89 Appendix A
Standard, 89 Appendix A
Standard Oil of California, 11, 94 Appendix B
Standard Register, 56, 95 Appendix B
Standardization, 37
Step, 89 Appendix A
Stiffness, 89 Appendix A
Stock Form, 89 Appendix A
Stored Output, 46
Stroke, 89 Appendix A
Stroke Analysis, 90 Appendix A
Stub, 90 Appendix A
STYLATOR, 12, 95 Appendix B

Substitution, 49, 90 Appendix A
Substitution Rates, 48, 90 Appendix A
Swedish Postal Bank (POSTGIRO), 27

Taplin Business Machines, 98 Appendix B
TAPPI, 90 Appendix A
Taube, Mortimer, 6
Tauschek, G., 93 Appendix B
Television Technology, 47
Template, 4
Template Matching, 4
Terminal, 90 Appendix A
Texas A & M University, 20
The Economics of OCR, 55
Thermal Printer, 90 Appendix A
Thickness, 90 Appendix A
Throughput, 90 Appendix A
Timing Mark, 90 Appendix A
Timing Track, 90 Appendix A
Tolerance, 90 Appendix A
Total Data Entry (TDE), 99 Appendix B
Trace, 98 Appendix B
Trace System, 59
Transaction Control and Encoding System, 59
Transistors, 47
Transmitted Light Scanner, 90 Appendix A
Transparent Inks, 90 Appendix A
Transport, 91 Appendix A
Transport Considerations, 51
Transport Design, 18
Transport Mechanism, 45
Transports, 46
Trim System, 60
Turnaround Document, 91 Appendix A
Type and Scan, 91 Appendix A
Typefont, 91 Appendix A
Types of Fonts, 47

UARCO, 56, 95 Appendix B
Ultraviolet Response, 91 Appendix A
Unit Set, 91 Appendix A

United Airlines, 27, 96 Appendix B
United States Air Force, 12, 17, 95 Appendix B
U.S. Army Finance Center, 28
U.S. Post Office Department, 17, 19, 95 Appendix B
United States Postal Service, 11, 58
UNIVAC's, 37
Universal Product Code, 91 Appendix A
University of Texas, 25
Upper Case, 91 Appendix A
USASI, 38
USASI-A Font, 34, 37

Variable Data, 91 Appendix A
Verify, 91 Appendix A
Vertical Field Separators, 91 Appendix A
Video Terminal Key Entry, 43
Vidicon Tubes, 47
Visible Response, 91 Appendix A
Vocabulary, 91 Appendix A
Void, 91 Appendix A

WAND Reader, 60
WAND Reader Terminals, 100 Appendix B
WAND Scanner, 91 Appendix A
Washington Daily News, 8
Weaver, A., 4, 93 Appendix B
Web, 91 Appendix A
Western Joint Computer Conference, 21, 96 Appendix B
White Standard, 91 Appendix A
Whither OCR, 33
Width, 91, Appendix A
Wire Side, 91 Appendix A
Word Processing, 92 Appendix A
Write Test, 92 Appendix A

ZIP Code, 65
ZIP Code Sorting System, 99 Appendix B
Zero Balance, 92 Appendix A
Zero Suppression, 92 Appendix A